Jenni Williams is Tutor in Old Testament at Wycliffe Hall, Oxford, and Associate Minister of St Peter's Church, Wootton. She is author of the article 'Tough Texts: Reading the parts we'd rather not' (*Anvil*, 2007), the chapter 'Deuteronomy' in *Tamar's Tears: Evangelical engagements with feminist hermeneutics* (Wipf & Stock, 2011), edited by Andrew Sloane, and *Reading Deuteronomy* (Grove Books, 2012). Dr Williams lives in Oxfordshire with her husband and two children.

GOD REMEMBERED RACHEL

Women's stories in the Old Testament and why they matter

JENNI WILLIAMS

First published in Great Britain in 2014

Society for Promoting Christian Knowledge
36 Causton Street
London SW1P 4ST
www.spckpublishing.co.uk

British Library Cataloguing-in-Publication Data
A catalogue record for this book is available from the British Library

ISBN 978–0–281–06684–1
eBook ISBN 978–0–281–06685–8

Typeset by Graphicraft Limited, Hong Kong
First printed in Great Britain by Ashford Colour Press
Subsequently digitally printed in Great Britain

eBook by Graphicraft Limited, Hong Kong

Produced on paper from sustainable forests

For
Jon, Danny and Ellie,
with love

Contents

Introduction

'I'm not doing the first reading,' announced the choir member. This is disconcerting to hear when you are helping out in a strange church while they are without a Vicar. 'It's sexist,' she continued, 'why should I?' My friend in the choir was not particularly trying to be difficult. She had read the story of Leah and Rachel and was honestly baffled by a world entirely alien from her own. These two ideas became part of the furniture of my study: *was* the Old Testament sexist and why *should* we read it?

This book is an attempt to look at the stories about women in the Old Testament and ask how stories about women can become part of our life journey in faith. If, as the Church has always believed, the Bible is the word of God, how can we as women use it to deepen our walk with God? The Old Testament was largely written by men in a very patriarchal society. Do these stories still matter for us?

Much of the Old Testament is cast as story. It speaks of people's lives and experiences of God. Many good approaches exist to explore how to appropriate biblical teaching for the life of the Church today. They seek an honest engagement with the Bible in a way that avoids the fundamentalist idea that it is simply a question of lifting practices off the page. A particularly good practical example of how to do this kind of engagement is Duvall and Hays' *Grasping God's Word*.[1] This book does not seek to do quite the same thing. Instead it explores stories and asks how simply reading and understanding those stories can speak into our lives and experiences; what we can learn about God and people from the narratives of people long ago. It also thinks about departure points for reflecting on how these stories can connect with ours and inform our lives.

The method I have used might be described as watching authors at work. Authors make choices: what to include; what to leave out. They bring certain characters, certain events to the foreground for the reader to notice; choose certain words that have a resonance for readers; arrange events. They pay considerable attention to one thing a character does while barely mentioning another, and they do this in a way designed to convey a message. Looking at these aspects of authors' work is called narratology, and is a useful way to understand what they are trying to say. Sometimes authors explicitly say how they think the reader should interpret a story; sometimes they leave us to think things over. When they do not say explicitly that this is – or is not – how life ought to be, readers may still make inferences from the narrative choices an author has made. This book explores the stories in this way. It also engages with the work of feminist scholars looking at the texts. Many Christians become uneasy when they are told that a reading is 'feminist', and instantly assume this will mean hostile, not Christian and anti-men. In fact there are a range of feminist readings and beliefs. Globally the feminist readings I have engaged with here come from scholars of Christian faith, Jewish faith and no faith, and could simply be defined as ones that look at the stories and ask: 'What about the women?'

Sometimes this will be a difficult read, as I have included stories where women's lives end in loss or disaster. I have included them nevertheless because loss and disaster are part of the experience of women – and men – both then and now.

The stories in their time

There are two separate but related ideas we need to be aware of when considering the Old Testament authors and their view of women. The first is that the Old Testament was written over centuries in societies that were patriarchal; that is, when all visible authority structures belonged to men. There are some notable exceptions in particular times of crisis but by and large this was the shape of society. In a society of this nature women can – although they need not necessarily – find themselves significantly disadvantaged. Choices are limited, public power is reduced – Ruth in Chapter 2 is an example of this – and the view of men who live in such a society about women may be very negative or stereotyped. In this type of society the needs and desires of women will be subordinated to such ideals as, for example, the continuing of the father's name, the maintenance of a clear authority structure with the father of the household at the top, ensuring that established public authority structures are not threatened, the controlling of female sexuality by the male head of the household and so on. One of the questions this book will be asking about all this is: 'Does the Old Testament collude with patriarchal abuses, does it critique them or does it not really comment?' We will need to observe the difference between places where the Old Testament is prescriptive (says how life *should be*) and where it is only descriptive (says how life *is*). An example of the latter will be explored in Chapter 4, which deals with the Levite's concubine.

How men see women

A related idea to patriarchy is the rather clumsily named andro-centricity, which means talking or writing about things from a man's point of view. It has become very familiar now to talk about how all history is his-story, and this is as true of the Bible as any other book written primarily by men. The Old Testament speaks far more about men than it does about women. The women spoken of are often used as unpleasant metaphors (faithless wife, temptress) or described mainly by their sexual function (wife, mother). So the second question we need to ask of the Old Testament is this: 'Are the writers of the Old Testament capable of portraying women fairly?' By this I mean: 'Do the writers try to portray the women as real people or merely as stereotypes?'

Often in such a patriarchal society it is argued that women will be portrayed in very stereotypical ways. This could be for one of two reasons. The first is that the male authors believe in the stereotypes. For example, Athalya Brenner argues that the stories of women in Genesis reflect the author's view that women cannot get on together.[2] The second reason may be that the male authors have an agenda in promoting the stereotypes: their ideology seeks to make women behave in a particular way and so portrays them as acting in that way. So, for example, pictures of submissive women may be portrayed as the norm because the author is seeking to make submission the norm. Equally, women can be portrayed as a source of danger and a threat to individual men – for example the 'temptress' figure of Proverbs 7, who functions as a model of how women are not supposed to act. It may be that men in a patriarchal society are either not capable of drawing women fairly or choose not to for their own agenda. However, we cannot simply assume that either of these things is true.

It is true that the authors of the Old Testament as we have it were largely men[3] and that they lived in a largely patriarchal society. But that does not necessarily mean they were incapable of sympathizing with or valuing women. A modern equivalent might be the observation that although the UK newspaper *The Guardian* was reporting stories throughout the era of Prime Minister Margaret Thatcher, nobody would ever have thought of it as promoting a Thatcherite agenda! The intention of this book is to look at how the stories are constructed and see how the women are written about. If the women appear to be fully rounded characters we might say that the author is not portraying them in stereotypes. An example of this kind of discussion can be found in Chapter 1, which deals with Leah and Rachel. If they make choices that do not seem to serve the ends of patriarchal structures, we may say that their portrayal is not androcentric. We will see this kind of discussion with the book of Ruth.

As a part of this comes the question of 'F' voice.[4] This is a way of describing texts that may give a woman's viewpoint on the world. In its beginning the idea of 'F' voice was based on possible female authorship that survived or was glimpsable behind male editing. Later the idea was expanded to consider any text that seemed to give a more 'female' point of view, perhaps evidenced by aspects of women's lives in which men would be less involved. Or a text might be considered 'F' voice if it foregrounds women: where women are the main actors. Thus the idea of 'F' voice overlaps with the idea of whether or not a male author can portray a woman as more than a stereotype.

The story and the reader

With much of the Old Testament it is simply not possible to know who actually wrote it (the 'empirical author') or for whom it was actually written (the 'empirical reader'). The best we can do is construct from its pages an 'implied author' (what we can imagine this writer to be like) and an implied reader (the kind of person at whom the writing seems aimed). This is important because the expectations of the implied reader and ours may be different because we come from different worldviews. There are things the implied reader can understand that we may not, particularly at the level of language. There are things we find shocking that the implied reader might not, or perhaps would. What this book is looking to do is explore and identify the intention of the implied author, but also be aware of possible differing reactions between us as 'empirical reader' and the implied reader.

Feminist scholars sometimes use the term 'retrievable'. This means that if a story or a text can be stripped of an androcentric agenda, it can still have something positive to say to women.

So we will examine stories that really do seem to be androcentric and ask whether they are in any way retrievable. An example of this can be found in Chapter 7, which deals with the story of Deborah.

Finally, a word of warning. In any book of this kind the writer's beliefs – the ones she or he is aware of and those not yet fully examined – will colour how that writer reads the text. I have tried to examine closely the narrative strategies used by the biblical authors to build the story, but no one can do this neutrally. A writer can identify the strategies the Old Testament authors use, but how the writer then interprets those authors' intentions in using those strategies will not be entirely objective. It will come from the writer's own life experiences and beliefs. It is the nature of story that it appeals to the people we are: it may create an effect in me that it does not in you, and vice versa. I come to the Old Testament with views about it that you may or may not share. Often in biblical studies scholars talk about the 'lenses' through which we all read, and this term is a helpful one. As you read you will encounter what my lenses have shown me. I have explored these stories in the belief that they do have something to say to women that can be God's word to us. I want to look the difficult texts in the eye but I am intrinsically a loyalist – someone who believes in the Bible as the word of God – as a matter of faith, and a feminist as a matter of conviction. You should bear this in mind as you read. My hope is not that you are persuaded by my readings in their entirety but rather that the readings in this book stimulate you to your own reflections on how these stories still matter.

The Bible text used for quotations is taken from NRSV. Words have multiple shades of meaning and sometimes I have commented on a word where a slight nuance in translation has been identified by biblical scholars and has been helpful to the reading. Where this has been done I have used a phrase such as 'can also be understood as' to make the point clear. Obviously, where a word or words are emphasized in a scriptural quote, that emphasis is mine.

Where biblical characters have had name changes during their stories (such as Sarai and Abram), I have generally used the name in that stage of the story. So I have used 'Sarai' up until Genesis 17.15 and 'Sarah' after that.

Part 1
WOMEN

1

Leah and Rachel:
such devoted sisters?

Genesis 29—31

Sisters can be very close, but what if something comes between them? Leah and Rachel are two sisters caught in a wretched triangle. They are both married to Jacob, but he only wanted to be married to Rachel. He agreed to work for seven years to earn the right to marry her. He was tricked into being married to Leah by the women's scheming father, Laban (Gen. 29.25). The text says Rachel was beautiful. The word for Leah's eyes can be understood as 'delicate' (Gen. 29.17). This might mean 'weak' eyes or, as NRSV has interpreted it, 'lovely'. Either way, Jacob fell in love with the younger sister, Rachel, but Laban veiled the bride and Jacob married Leah. He found out too late and protested. Laban agreed to let him marry Rachel as well in return for another seven years' service. Jacob did not love Leah but it appears that Leah loved Jacob, or at least longed for genuine affection between them. Leah was able to bear children, apparently as a divine consolation for not being loved (Gen. 29.31) but Rachel is infertile as the episode we are considering begins. It does not take much to imagine the bitterness felt by Jacob, Leah and Rachel in such a difficult situation. What ensues is a competition between the sisters that becomes increasingly bitter as time goes on. They compete to bear children. The irony is that they do it from exactly opposite motivations. Leah believes that if she bears enough sons her husband will love her; Rachel knows that her husband loves her but her life is incomplete until she has had sons. Brenner argues that the story of Leah and Rachel and others like it show that the author thinks women cannot cooperate.

> The implications of such stories are that women cannot be friends even when they share an important common purpose, namely the continuity and preservation of the family unit . . . Even when they are sisters rivalry, jealousy, and insecurity are so great that any possibility of empathy or affection between sisters is excluded. Men are seen as different, much more mature socially.[1]

In this chapter we will consider whether the story of Leah and Rachel is indeed an illustration of the view that women cannot cooperate, that motherhood is everything and that women will do anything to achieve it.

The situation between Leah and Rachel is set up for a very particular 'type' of story, referred to by Brenner as the 'Hero's Mother'.[2] This story has certain predictable features:

- A woman is infertile for an extended period of time.
- She receives a divine promise of a change in her situation.
- She competes with another woman and is humiliated by her.
- The other woman in the household is usually inferior in some way.
- The competition is so fierce that neither woman can control it and even family welfare can be overshadowed by it.
- The woman cannot achieve personal security until she conceives.
- The two women cannot cooperate except in the face of an outside threat.
- The son born to the inferior woman is a false heir.

Brenner applies this 'type' of story to Sarah and Hagar, Rachel and Leah, and Hannah and Peninnah. Not all these features necessarily appear in all the stories, and it is often where the story breaks away from the type that it becomes most interesting. In this story of two sisters, Rachel is indeed infertile, apparently long enough for her to feel there is a problem (Gen. 30.1). There is no explicit divine promise, although there is an insistence that only God can give children (he 'opens' Leah's womb and later 'opens' Rachel's). Rachel and Leah do compete – the difference is that each of them feels humiliated or is humiliated, for different reasons. Leah is indeed 'inferior' in that she is less loved. However, some of the other features of the type break down. Most significant to our discussion is seeing how the story of Leah and Rachel is a story of how a relationship between sisters is broken by a devious man but later restored. The competition in the family is at quite a pitch but the women will learn to control it. The son of the 'inferior' woman is not a false heir (for at least one of them, Judah, will found the royal line of Israel). If final reconciliation does only come in the face of an outside threat (from their father), we will see that the seeds of the reconciliation are sown before.

The story is situated in the middle of a bigger story about deception: the life story of the ancestors. Abraham deceives two kings by pandering Sarah to gain safety (Gen. 12, 20); Isaac tries the same trick with Rebekah (Gen. 26). Jacob deceives his father to get the birthright blessing (Gen. 27); Laban deceives Jacob about which daughter he is marrying; Jacob deceives Laban about which of the flocks Laban should give him (Gen. 30); the sisters deceive their father about his household gods (Gen. 31); Jacob's sons deceive the man who raped their sister Dinah (Gen. 34) and then deceive Jacob about the faked death of Joseph (Gen. 37); Joseph deceives his brothers about a stolen cup and his identity (Gen. 44). A maelstrom of connivance swirls around Abram's family from almost the very moment the Lord promises them blessing. At one level many of the stories deal with how all these deceptions are exposed and resolved. What is interesting in the story we are examining is that although the initial deception is set up by a man, the author shows us the fallout in the lives of two women and how the women come to terms with the wretched situation in which they find themselves.

There is a very noticeable narrative dynamic in Genesis 29—31 in the way both Leah and Rachel move forwards and backwards on the stage of the narrative, allowing each of them time and space to tell her own story in her speeches. In this way the author allows their actions to become understandable to the reader as their states of mind are articulated. The stories of the two sisters are intertwined by more than a common husband: they are intertwined by the fact that each of them wants what the other has. And they are intertwined by a common anger: Leah resents the fact that Rachel is the preferred wife and Rachel resents Leah's ability to have children. In this next section we will look at Leah and Rachel as they speak of what they feel.

Leah's story

Leah has done the thing her society expects of her: she has given her husband sons. This gives her status in her community. According to many biblical scholars, including Brenner above, she should feel happy or at least secure because children are the great desire of women as portrayed in the Bible. But her story is the story of a desire for love. We should not interpret this as romantic love, which after all cannot simply happen to order. It is more likely that Jacob is failing to offer Leah the affection and respect expected in a society that arranges its marriages – not romantic love, but caring. The fate of the unloved wife is the next episode in the story, and Leah moves centre stage.

Leah's fertility is the Lord's consolation for the way she is treated, as we saw. She names her sons to convey her hopes and feelings. This seems to be a time where the mother names her sons (Jacob only intervenes to keep Benjamin from a 'bad luck' name in Gen. 35.18). The first son is called Reuben (which sounds like 'see, a son!'), 'for she said, "Because the LORD has looked on my affliction; surely now my husband will love me"' (Gen. 29.32). For Jacob did not 'see' her on her wedding day until it was too late. But she feels the Lord has 'seen' her. The birth of the second son, Simeon (whose name sounds like 'hear'), again shows that Leah feels the Lord is involved in her life, yet still she defines her being by her husband's feeling towards her: 'She conceived again and bore a son, and said, "Because the LORD has heard that I am hated, he has given me this son also"' (Gen. 29.33). It is interesting that for these first two children there are these two aspects to the naming: one is a feeling about Jacob, the other an expression of praise to the Lord. The third son, Levi (whose name speaks of 'joining'), shows that she still wants a better relationship with Jacob: 'Again she conceived and bore a son, and said, "Now this time my husband will be joined to me, because I have borne him three sons"' (Gen. 29.34). Leah does not mention the Lord this time. The author, by focusing only on her doomed hopes, creates a crescendo of Leah's feeling about Jacob. But doomed is exactly what her hope is: by the fourth son she seems to have become aware that Jacob will never be 'joined' to her. For this fourth son represents a shift: Judah ('praise') is her final child at this point, and she seems only to think about the Lord who has given her children: 'She conceived again and bore a son, and said, "This time I will praise the LORD"' (Gen. 29.35). Leah seems to be moving away from her focus on Jacob and relying more on the Lord who never failed her even if her husband did. But if she has stopped hoping for Jacob's love, she still sees her status as wife as important, as we shall see.

Leah stops having children – the text does not tell us why. Perhaps Jacob stopped sleeping with her. This explanation is supported by Leah's reaction when she meets the desperate Rachel in the fields later in the story. She answers Rachel's pleading with the bitter 'Is it a small matter that you have taken away my husband?' (Gen. 30.15). That it was simply a question of Jacob stopping sleeping with her is reinforced by the ease with which Leah seems to get pregnant after one night (Gen. 30.17). On the other hand, she may have experienced what we would now call secondary infertility. This would explain why she gives her maid to Jacob to sleep with (Gen. 30.9). The text says that she did this because she realized she had stopped bearing children. If this is the case, her rebuke to Rachel is not about sexual contact but about affection: she feels that the marital affection to which she has a right has been absorbed by Jacob's feelings for her sister.

In such a situation Leah is as prepared as Rachel to get involved in a childbearing race. Both Leah and Rachel have presented Jacob with a maid to provide yet more heirs. What is clear is that Leah is not portrayed as secure even though she has four sons. Leah's maid Zilpah bears her two surrogate children, Gad ('good fortune') and Asher ('happy'): 'Happy am I! For the women will call me happy' (Gen. 30.13). Not only has she stopped looking at Jacob, Leah seems to have stopped looking at the Lord as well. Increasingly she does not look for love but for status as a woman blessed with children. The bargain in the fields is sealed: mandrakes – thought to promote fertility – for Rachel; another night with Jacob for Leah. Leah recognizes there is no romance for her in all this: the son born after this night is called Issachar ('hire'). Then another son, Zebulun ('dowry'): 'God has endowed me with a good dowry; now my husband will honour me, because I have borne him six sons' (Gen. 30.20). These words are about contractual obligation and business. She no longer looks for love, only 'honour'. Yet at the same time Leah again speaks of God: he has enabled her to conceive again. Then comes Dinah, whose name has – apparently – no significance. Leah has given up on Jacob except as a means to an end. Her unrequited love has finally grown cold. The process by which this has happened has been portrayed to us through the names of her children and the explanation for each name.

Rachel's story

Rachel, on the other hand, has the love of her husband who works not seven but fourteen years to get her. He may have had sex with her sister for seven years and given her children, but 'he loved Rachel more than Leah' (Gen. 29.30). But no children come. The Lord opens Leah's womb, but the opposite phrase for Rachel is absent, instead she is 'infertile' (Gen. 29.31). There are other examples of women where the phrase 'the Lord closed her womb' are used and we will explore this with Hannah, but with Rachel the phrase is not used. Of course, to the ancient author the Lord makes everything happen, so it would have been understood that he did not give Rachel children. It may be that choosing not to use the parallel pair 'open her womb'/ 'close her womb' is the author's hint that God is not punishing Rachel: he simply does not give her children.

Rachel comes centre stage as the next episode begins and, like Leah, is given time to tell us how her experiences make her feel. Rachel finds her infertility unbearable: 'Give me children, or I shall die!' (Gen. 30.1). Jacob does not understand the issue: there are sons in the family, so there is no problem – there are heirs enough to continue the line and support the family in his old age. Jacob's response expresses both what the author saw as a fundamental truth – only God can grant fertility – and also the exasperation of a husband who feels his womenfolk are being too demanding: 'Jacob became very angry with Rachel and said, "Am I in the place of God, who has withheld from you the fruit of the womb?"' (Gen. 30.2). Jacob's voice, just like Elkanah's, which we will explore in Chapter 10, is the voice of patriarchy. Some scholars have criticized Rachel's lack of piety because she does not pray but goes straight to practical action. At any rate, Rachel chooses the same route as her grandmother-in-law Sarai: surrogacy. Rachel gives her slave Bilhah to Jacob to sleep with and then names the two sons born to her. Just like Leah, she names the first one (Dan: 'he judged') with reference to God: 'God has judged me, and has also heard my voice and given me a son' (Gen. 30.6). We have seen that Leah named her first two sons with both God's attention to her plight and her desire for Jacob's love in mind. Rachel is not shown as anxious about Jacob's love – she already has it. But the naming of Bilhah's second son should bring us pause. Up until now the story has not spoken explicitly of the jealousy between the sisters. Leah's namings were about God and Jacob – they did not speak explicitly of how she felt about Rachel. But Rachel names Naphtali ('wrestle') because she thinks she has 'won'. 'With mighty wrestlings I have wrestled with my sister, and have prevailed' (Gen. 30.8). But the story will go on to show that surrogacy has not made her happy, any more than it did Sarah – whose experience is corrupted by jealousy, as we will see in Chapter 3. For Rachel, although Bilhah's children do not seem to be a cause of jealousy or disharmony between her and the maid, surrogacy has not assuaged her longing to give birth to a child herself. The next time we see Rachel, she is seeking for a medical remedy for infertility, as we will see below. But as Brenner notes in the 'type' discussed above, even this is not enough: the birth of Joseph ('he adds') triggers only the desire for more sons: 'and she named him Joseph, saying, "May the LORD add to me another son!"' (Gen. 30.24). But for the moment, no more children come.

We might pause at this moment in recognition of the two women who do not get a voice at all: Bilhah and Zilpah. We will look in detail in a later chapter at Hagar, the first slave to bear a surrogate child in Genesis; she is given two scenes in which to describe how she feels. These two are not. Perhaps they found their lives bearable. However, these slaves do not have a say in being used this way: their bodies belong to their 'mistresses'. It is worth noting that the Old Testament recognizes a category of woman called the slave-wife, who is acquired for childbearing but treated as a secondary wife and has certain safeguards about her experience in the family: she cannot be sent away at her husband's whim and gets certain material luxuries in food and clothing that mark her as different from a household slave (Exod. 21.7–11). It may be that this was the experience of Bilhah and Zilpah but the text does not say. So in their case they become known as Jacob's 'women': people with whom he has a recognized sexual relationship (Gen. 31.17), although they are not regarded as wives in the same way as Leah and Rachel. Nonetheless, the author chooses not to voice these women or tell us anything about their lives.

The sisters' stories

After Rachel arranges for children through surrogacy, Leah copies her. Leah calls one of her surrogate children Asher ('happy'), but as the stories of Rachel and Leah converge, we see that she is no more happy than Rachel was as the last scene closed. The first scene where both of them are front stage begins in conflict and ends in a grudging agreement. The second scene sees the sisters united against a common enemy: their father. After this the relationship between the sisters is backgrounded – the only mentions of them are in relation to Jacob or Laban.

To return to the first scene: Leah meets Rachel in the fields and both of them are allowed to express their bitter unhappiness. Rachel is simply desperate to have a child. Although she has felt in competition with Leah, now she is desperate enough to bury her pride and beg Leah for a source of fertility: mandrakes. Leah's journey has apparently come from the other direction: where first she focused on Jacob as the source of her unhappiness, now her rage against Rachel bursts out (Gen. 30.15). But although the power dynamic between them seems unbalanced, with Rachel begging and Leah furious, actually they both very quickly come to understand they each might have power over the other. Rachel apparently has the power to persuade Jacob to sleep with Leah, and Leah's son – another marker of her fertility, the thing Rachel has not – has the mandrakes that may bring fertility to Rachel. There is a subtle symmetry here. Apparently the tension between the two women is at least lessened as they realize that a truce and cooperation can benefit them both. 'Each gives up her particular prerogative in order to gain the prize she lacks.'[3] They have learnt that trade is better than war. We might pause here and consider that this is an example of the cooperation that Brenner thought the author did not show. The sisters are not reconciled but they can – however reluctantly – cooperate without threat for mutual benefit.

At another level this interchange is a surprising and ludicrous scene. It is surprising because in a world where the sexuality of women is controlled by men, two women can apparently barter for a man's sexuality. It is ludicrous because, with not one but two maidservants presented to Jacob for impregnation, he begins to look less like the head of his household and more like the parish bull. This episode also indicates the reality of the gulf between authority and power. Jacob is the head of his household but he finds himself instructed by women about whom he should sleep with. Most surprisingly of all, the author draws back from making value judgements about the women's use of power.

The sisters seemed to discover that they both had the power to offer something to each other and get what they wanted in return. But fertility (for Rachel) and affection (for Leah) are not to be had for the taking. Both think they can give the other what she needs, but neither has the power they hoped towards the other, even if they can get Jacob to do what they want. For the mandrakes do not heal Rachel and, from the names she gave her two new sons, Leah found her renewed sexual encounter with Jacob somewhat less than joyful, as we saw above. The birth of a daughter, not even given a naming-story, is even less remarked on. The dismantling of the deal the sisters contracted is an awareness of the limitations of their power over each other. Rachel will only conceive when *God* remembers her. And if Jacob consents to sleep with Leah, no power on earth or heaven, it seems, can compel him to show affection to his first wife. The author does not tell us how the women reflected on the outcome of their trade, but there are hints in Leah's naming of her sons and daughter and also Rachel's reaction to the birth of Joseph ('add'): it seems her thirst for children is not quenched but made worse. Each looked for a solution from that meeting in the field; neither found it.

By the second scene in which they appear together, the sisters appear to have put down their antagonism and have learned not to blame each other, but to put the blame where it truly lies: on the father who used both of them. Their intolerable situation was created by Laban, as they now acknowledge.

> Then Rachel and Leah answered him, 'Is there any portion or inheritance left to us in our father's house? Are we not regarded by him as foreigners? For he has sold us, and he has been using up the money given for us. (Gen. 31.14–15)

The author has them speaking with one voice, which is significant. Leah and Rachel have been reconciled, at least in the matter of how they got into the situation, and they agree to work with Jacob to resolve it. This outside threat is not entirely the reason they drop their differences, not according to the logic of the story that has been building towards this moment. The author has allowed Leah and Rachel a journey in the story, through competition and bitterness and even hatred, through reluctant cooperation to reconciliation, at least partly.

We do not know whether there was then complete peace between the sisters because any mention of either of them after this is in relation to a man: either Jacob or Laban.

Their final fates are slightly different. Rachel dies, and her tragedy is that it is the thing she wanted so badly that kills her. 'Give me children or I shall die' becomes 'Give me children and I shall die'. However, her story is not entirely pathetic, as she shows in the episode of stealing Laban's gods and either menstruating on them – a terrible insult – or using her menstruation as a way to deceive her father (Gen. 31.34–35). Rachel is not just a victim. Leah's life also has its share of tragedy and loss. Her daughter Dinah is raped and her life destroyed by brothers bent on revenge (Gen. 34). The order in which Jacob sends his various families ahead of him in a potentially dangerous meeting with Esau shows he still prefers Rachel: he keeps her and Joseph until last. Rachel is built a tomb of her own but, poignantly, it is Leah who will be buried in the tomb of Jacob's family, an important place where he himself wishes to be buried. Jacob refers to the tomb as the resting place of Abraham, Sarah, Isaac and Rebekah, then adds 'and there I buried Leah' (Gen. 49.31). He chooses to end his story where Leah's story ended.

The author of the story of Jacob's family portrays carefully the journey of Leah and Rachel's relationship. Certainly that relationship will in many ways mirror the jealousies and rivalries between the sons who will make up the tribes of Israel, whose stories we cannot go into here. But by voicing the two sisters so fully, the author allows us to watch two women put in an impossible situation. So interpreting their relationship becomes more complex and demanding than the 'type' suggests. It seems to me that the author is allowing us to see that when women are forced into this toxic situation of two women and one man, conflict is inevitable but not irresolvable. When women are forced to compete for male approval, in whatever form, it will damage the relationship between them. The author shows how two women can rebuild their relationship, painfully and perhaps not fully. This story gives us hope that there may be a way to repair the damage. It comes when both women recognize the limitations of whatever power they have and that God is the final decider of their fate. They become more than simply wives: they create other relationships and other connections. However, whatever sisterhood they may have recovered does not apparently extend to the maids. We will explore the question of another woman who had to serve as surrogate, Hagar, in Chapter 9.

Conflict between people in the Church inevitably creates a group whom we might call 'collateral damage': people who get sucked in on one side or the other and end up against each other in a conflict they never started. The story of Leah and Rachel shows both the cost of this experience and the need to focus on God and our own need of him as a way to rebuild. This should not be said glibly: repairing heartfelt damage is a painful process in which both sides will always have to sacrifice a little of their own feelings of grievance.

For reflection

- Do you think the sisters were able to be reconciled?
- Do you think the author offers an implicit critique of men who use women?
- What effect does it have on the voicing of Leah and Rachel that Bilhah and Zilpah are silent?
- Why do you think Dinah is given no 'naming story'?
- How can women build one another up?

2

Ruth: lean on me

Ruth 1—4

The story of Ruth begins in a series of losses. Famine in Bethlehem brings an Israelite family to Moab. The sons are married to Moabite women. Elimelech, the father of the household, dies, then the two sons. All that is left of the family of Elimelech are his widow, Naomi, and the widows of his sons, Ruth and Orpah. In terms of the continuance of the house of Elimelech, all is apparently lost, for both young couples have not had children. Naomi has truly lost everything she cares about (Ruth 1.5). She even seems to have lost God, whom she now sees as a threatening force in her life:

> She said to them, 'Call me no longer Naomi [pleasant], call me Mara [bitter], for the Almighty has dealt bitterly with me. I went away full, but the Lord has brought me back empty; why call me Naomi when the Lord has dealt harshly with me, and the Almighty has brought calamity upon me?'   (Ruth 1.20–21)

From Naomi's point of view the household of Elimelech cannot stay together. At one level she is realistic: she cannot produce more sons for the women to marry. She is even generous: she cannot expect them to uproot from their communities for her sake and face an uncertain future in Israel, which is her only choice. Both daughters-in-law protest their loyalty to Naomi and offer to return to Israel (Ruth 1.10). Clearly in the past this has been a relationship of mutual affection. But Naomi is firm that they must go home to their own families. If they do that, the usual social mechanisms will reassert themselves: their fathers will try to find them other husbands. Naomi even offers a blessing, underlining the fact that this is an ending.[1] These days we might call it 'closure' – an ending that leaves everybody at peace, even if sad. Orpah, one of the daughters-in-law, is persuaded after a while to follow Naomi's advice. Ruth insists on going with Naomi back to Bethlehem. Ironically, the name of the town from which Elimelech fled in time of famine is 'House of Bread' and, as if to underline the desolation and loss of Naomi, they arrive at harvest in a time of fertility in the land. In Bethlehem Ruth goes out into the fields after the harvesters to 'glean'; that is, to pick up whatever the harvesters may have left, so she and Naomi can survive. Ruth finds herself in the field of a kindly man called Boaz who protects her and helps her. Naomi tells Ruth that Boaz is a 'kinsman-redeemer', someone who is responsible for the welfare of the wider family of Elimelech. She tells Ruth to wait until the night after the threshing, go and lie down at Boaz's feet as he lies in his barn and wait to see what he will do. Ruth goes, and when Boaz awakes in the morning she asks again for his protection. Boaz agrees to marry her but must first outwit a closer relative who could claim her if he wished. The story ends happily when Ruth and Boaz are married and Naomi has a grandson who brings her great joy. From this family comes the line of King David.

Everybody in society has roles to play, roles we are expected to fulfil. Those roles can be more or less constricting, more or less oppressive, but every society has them. One of the most beloved books in the history of English literature is surely Jane Austen's *Pride and Prejudice*. What makes it so delightful is the character of Elizabeth Bennet, who somehow manages to be sparkling, witty and perceptive yet also willing to allow her perceptions to be challenged. She is not cynical but nor is she naive in the way her sister Jane is. Elizabeth dances her way through human relations, somehow conveying a sense of freedom. She is irresistible. Yet she is situated in Jane Austen's time when women were decidedly not free. Their roles, although different, were as closely dictated as in biblical times and the punishment for transgressing a boundary was pitiless. Tony Tanner provides an excellent answer to the apparent paradox of Elizabeth's willingness to fulfil her roles and her refusal to allow them to dictate to her: role distance. People who have role distance will carry out the roles society assigns to them but will not allow themselves to be defined by them. Where they perceive those roles as unfair or ridiculous they will refuse to follow them: Elizabeth's refusal to give the socially superior Lady Catherine de Bourgh her way is a good example.[2] She is the kind of person who 'may often wish to make a gesture of disengagement from the roles he is called on to play, to indicate that he has not become mindlessly imprisoned in those roles'.[3] In this chapter we look at Ruth, a biblical woman who within the confines of her society managed to do very much the same.

Love and loyalty

From the very beginning of Ruth's story she is always doing things contrary to expectation. As we have seen, Naomi insists that the daughters-in-law have no realistic future with her and should go home. Orpah, evidently a generous girl but with a certain amount of 'common sense', protests once and then takes her leave regretfully. Orpah is the Charlotte Lucas of the piece: warm, affectionate but realistic. A Moabite Mr Collins is her best hope and she recognizes it. The biblical author does not criticize Orpah for following the roles her society has set up for her. As Katharine Sakenfeld points out, the effect of Orpah's actions is to underline how 'extraordinary' Ruth's loyalty to Naomi really is.[4]

We have noted the importance of dialogue in the story of Rachel and Leah, and here too Ruth's speech is both vital to understand the plot and indicative of the author's perspective. Ellen van Wolde observes that Ruth is invisible in her society because she is no longer wife-of, or daughter-of relative to a man, only to a woman who is herself no longer connected in these terms.[5] But the author wants to make the invisible visible and does it by allowing Ruth to speak, to explain her motivations.

What Orpah does is what is expected of Ruth. Naomi expects it; the implied reader would have expected it too. Women should settle down, marry and produce children. Family, tribal and clan loyalties are strong. But Ruth's choice is different. She chooses not marriage but sisterhood – she attaches herself to Naomi with an impassioned declaration of what that will mean: Naomi's land, Naomi's people, Naomi's God (Ruth 1.16–17). There is a repeated use of the word 'turn' in this first chapter of Ruth that creates a sense of movement. But because the word seems to be used by Naomi as a way of saying 'return to your mother's house' (Ruth 1.8, 11, 12, 15) and by Ruth to mean 'do not ask me to turn from you' and 'do not ask me to change my mind' (Ruth 1.10, 16), the direction of the turning is every which way. This then creates a sense of unease, even menace. The reader coming to the story for the first time wonders what is the safest, the wisest thing to do. The author wants readers to ask themselves where Ruth should turn.

Belonging

Ruth knows what is expected of her but she recognizes there might be something more important. Scholars have variously interpreted her devotion as sisterhood (devotion to Naomi) or as a recognition of Israel's God (a desire to be a part of the covenant people). But in my view the story suggests that what the author wants to show is devotion to Naomi. For Ruth it means risking not being able to carry out the traditional woman's role. It is difficult for us as readers to appreciate this because we know the end of the story. From Ruth's point of view the choice she has made makes it extremely unlikely that she will ever marry and have children. This is because Ruth will be moving to a place where she is a foreigner dependent on a pauper. More problematically still for the historical context in which she is set, she is not only a foreigner but a Moabite. Prejudice about Moabites ran deep in Israel: it was believed that they were born of an incestuous relationship (Gen. 19.36–37), and Deuteronomy banned them for ten generations from the assembly of Israel because of the way they treated Israel earlier in its history (Deut. 23.3–5). Moab was, of course, a cousin nation to Israel through Abraham's nephew Lot, and there is no bitterness quite like the bitterness of that kind of connection. The drama and risk of Ruth's choice are underlined at every turn.

When Naomi and Ruth arrive in Bethlehem, Naomi stays in whatever house she and Ruth have managed to find. It is Ruth who goes out in public, Ruth whose gleaning proclaims their destitution to the world. Ruth takes the initiative: someone must do something or they will both starve. But her choice is not without risk: bad things can happen to solitary women out in the fields. This is especially true of a foreign woman known to be without a male protector.

Into this potentially difficult situation comes a male protector: a decent – if rather paternalistic – man called Boaz. Boaz seems to recognize Ruth's choice in staying with Naomi as one to be admired, for he will later refer to it as *hesed*, a word famously difficult to translate but one of the defining qualities of God himself. Some translate it 'loyalty', others 'mercy'. Personally I think this is one of the times when the King James translation of this word in the book of Psalms, 'lovingkindness', best conveys what it is. At any rate, Boaz applauds Ruth's *hesed* to Naomi. He seems to feel that this devotion makes Ruth entitled to the attention and care of God himself: 'May the LORD reward you for your deeds, and may you have a full reward from the LORD, the God of Israel, under whose wings you have come for refuge!' (Ruth 2.12).

Throughout many of the biblical writings such as Deuteronomy and the prophets, three groups of people are particularly to be looked after by the people of Israel, as being especially under the eye of God: widows, orphans and the stranger (Deut. 10.17–18). Part of the covenant as expressed in the laws of Deuteronomy is to look after these groups, and those who did not were considered as deserving of the Lord's anger (Deut. 27.19). So Ruth, widow and stranger, has come under the covenant by a son of Israel declaring the Lord's protection over her.

Boaz does more than utter pious sentiment, though. He ensures that Ruth will be unmolested, provides her with food, suggests that if she takes a little more than she is entitled to, his workers should turn a blind eye to it, and finally suggests they should arrange for a little more barley to be available for gleaning than would be usual. It may be paternalism, but it is also a lifeline for two destitute, unprotected women.

Naomi's reaction to this unsuspected support is one of huge relief: 'Where did you glean today? And where have you worked? Blessed be the man who took notice of you' (Ruth 2.19). Naomi voices the point of view of a patriarchal society: a male authority figure is what is needed.

Ruth's perspective on Boaz again indicates her ability to create distance between her accepted role and her own ability to think for herself. She is grateful, of course. When Boaz makes his offer of protection in the field, she says what she must: 'Then she said, "May I continue to find favour in your sight, my lord, for you have comforted me and spoken kindly to your servant, even though I am not one of your servants"' (Ruth 2.13). She does not know at this stage that Boaz is related to Elimelech's family: she knows of no claim on him. So from her perspective a decent man has offered his help. Therefore at one level this is just the response that a dependant without claim should give to someone who offers their patronage. Yet a little gentle irony is allowed into her speech: she is *not* one of his servants. In saying she is not one of his servants she has also freed herself slightly from binding social hierarchies, even at the same time as she is saying what is socially appropriate. Her place in the hierarchy is fixed yet she is not bound by it. Ruth will not be limited by the role of social inferior, and here she lays down her verbal marker to that effect: she has role distance.

Love, loyalty and risk

Naomi is the one to move the plot on in the next scene. She wants Ruth to have security and be well (Ruth 3.1). To Naomi the role of wife will achieve this end. She tells Ruth that Boaz is *go'el* (kin redeemer). This reflects a law about a rescuer (Lev. 25.25) who steps in during situations of extreme poverty to make sure a family member is not utterly destitute. Boaz will restore the lives of Naomi and Ruth. But Naomi's plan is oblique. Perhaps this reflects Ruth's status as poor Moabite and therefore not a desirable wife, or perhaps it simply indicates how difficult it was for a woman to get things like betrothals settled without a man. Naomi's plan has huge risk. Ruth is to wait until Boaz is drunk and asleep, strip his lower half and lie down beside him. After this, when he wakes up, says Naomi, Boaz will tell Ruth what to do (Ruth 3.4). Ruth promises to do all that Naomi tells her. There has been a good deal of discussion about whether or not Boaz and Ruth actually have sex that night. Some Christians find it difficult to contemplate a heroine who would seduce a man this way and so tend to insist that nothing happened. Others tend to think there can only be one outcome when a woman strips a half-drunk, half-asleep man. But from the point of view of the risk Ruth is taking, it does not matter whether they actually had sex because the very fact that she spent the night next to him means that, if the community hears about her presence that night, it will be assumed that they did have sex. Ruth only had one thing going for her in Israel: her reputation as a woman who lived her life within sexual bounds. If Boaz chooses not to offer her his protection (marriage or concubinage or some other form of recognized status), this will all be lost. So this choice to do as Naomi says is, in some ways, even more risky than her choice not to go home to her mother's house. Up to this point everyone has apparently been admiring her noble loyalty (Ruth 2.11). After this night, they might publicly condemn her as morally compromised and possibly have all their previous prejudices about Moabites confirmed. Everything hangs on Boaz's decision the next day.

Role distance

But the next day does not work out quite as Naomi has planned. In her mind, indeed in her world, men make decisions, so it is for Boaz to take the next step (Ruth 3.4). But Ruth again shows her capacity to distance herself from the role – this time the role of a woman who waits to be asked. She told Naomi she would follow her instructions but instead she takes the initiative and does not wait for Boaz's decision. 'He said, "Who are you?" And she answered, "I am Ruth, your servant; spread your cloak over your servant, for you are next-of-kin"' (Ruth 3.9). As many scholars have noted, the last time the expression 'spread your cloak over' was heard, it was in the field where Boaz was blessing Ruth with the wish that the Lord, the God of Israel, would spread his wings over her – the word for cloak and wings is the same (Ruth 2.12). Instead of waiting for Boaz to decide her destiny, Ruth effectively brings his own words back to him and suggests that he, Boaz, is the chosen means of that said protection. There is something about this that is gently comic without ever being socially threatening: it would make an Israelite audience laugh rather than see Ruth as a threat to social order. She has been able to distance herself from her role but does not reject it. Boaz says to Ruth, 'I will do for you all that you ask' (Ruth 3.11). This echoes Ruth's promise to Naomi, 'All that you tell me I will do' (Ruth 3.5). But just as Ruth chose her own way to go about things, so will Boaz. It is he who will act – he who will go to the gate and deal with the nearer kinsman-redeemer. Boaz may allow a woman to take control in private – what happens in public is patriarchal.

Ruth's action is not in any way binding on Boaz. But one of the things that make this story so delightful is that Boaz can do role distance as well. Something in him responds to Ruth. His speech shows that he has understood what she has done. He says that what she has done, even though she has stepped outside bounds, is *hesed*. She is a 'worthy woman' (Ruth 3.11). He makes sure the closer relative will not pursue his claim so that Boaz himself can have Ruth, but he will act within the rules. Ironically, he will have to be oblique in the way Ruth and Naomi have been, to ensure he can manoeuvre the closer relative out of the running. Like Ruth, Boaz does not question the roles their society sets down for them; it is just that both are willing to circumvent them a little if necessary.

So Boaz meets at the gate with the closer relative. His name is only given as 'friend' – much as we might say 'Whatsisname'. Boaz tells him that Naomi has a field to be redeemed. At first keen to acquire Naomi's field, Whatsisname excuses himself when presented with the additional commitment to Ruth (Ruth 4.6). He renounces his right to be kinsman-redeemer and takes off his sandal to confirm the transaction with Boaz – the author tells us that this was a standard way of doing business in Israel (Ruth 4.7). But it also irresistibly reminds the reader of the one place in biblical law where a woman is allowed to enact the law. In Deuteronomy, if a family member will not marry the childless widow of a brother, she is allowed publicly to shame him by spitting in his face, and he removes his sandal. His family is then known as 'the house of him whose sandal was pulled off' – marked for ever as hardhearted and ignoring the spirit of the Law (Deut. 25.5–10).

Shaming in ancient Israel had an impact on people that is difficult to appreciate in modern Western society: it was a very serious sanction. In the episode here, Whatsisname, in taking off his sandal, effectively shames himself. The author's opinion of him is clear by the fact that his name has been left out. One of the purposes of the law in Deuteronomy was to keep the dead man's name going. This would happen by the first son being named as son of the dead man. In our story, Whatsisname's refusal does not result in the loss of Mahlon's name – Mahlon was Ruth's husband – but the loss of his own. So the story allows a subversion of belongingness and role: one of 'us' (the Israelite Whatsisname) refuses to honour the spirit of the law; one of 'them' (the Moabite), by her loyalty to Naomi and her God, 'is portrayed as the example of what loyal Israelite living ought to be like'.[6]

So the characters of Ruth and Boaz are set up as perfect for each other, for they have the same outlook on life, roles and morality. The blessing pronounced by the male elders indicates Ruth's character well: that she should be like the women who built the 12 tribes and that Boaz's house should be like that of his ancestor Perez (Ruth 4.11–12). This last reinforces the author's portrayal of Ruth's capacity for role distance, for the allusion is to Tamar, Judah's daughter-in-law who stepped outside the boundaries of accepted sexual roles in order to achieve her ends. Indeed, it is often noted by Christians that only four women are mentioned in the genealogy of Jesus (Matt. 1.3–6) and three of them are remembered for stepping outside the boundaries of acceptable female behaviour in the cause of a greater good. We should not push this too far as one of the women is Bathsheba, who is a victim of a man's out-of-bounds action. Nevertheless, the idea that three women who did step outside boundaries should be remembered as part of the story is a helpful perspective.

There is also a reference to Rachel and Leah. In some ways the story of Ruth is the healing of the story of Rachel and Leah. These two women, Naomi and Ruth, do not compete but do what they can for each other. Naomi is very much defined by her roles and does not think outside them or critique them. But within her roles she is generally kind to Ruth in a way Leah and Rachel had to struggle to achieve. The circumstances of their lives drove Leah and Rachel apart. In the story of Ruth we have the story of two women whose life circumstances are unable to break the bond of sisterhood.

The story of Ruth has a happy ending for everyone. Naomi, subsumed still in her in roles, has what she wanted: she belongs to a family and has a grandson (Ruth 4.15). Ruth and Boaz, as we have seen, have been set up to be seen as a good match with a genuine connection between them. As Darcy in *Pride and Prejudice* is capable of role distance (marrying a social inferior, refusing the engagement arranged by his aunt and mother), so Boaz can see past 'foreignness' to genuine worth. The clans of Abraham that were separated in Genesis 13 come back together.[7]

We have seen the significance of the male elders' blessing, but the last word goes to the village women, who act as a chorus telling us the way the author interprets the characters. Naomi has a 'son' – that was what she wanted. But Ruth, astonishingly, is declared to be better for Naomi than seven sons (Ruth 4.15). Her devotion to another woman is the last thing we hear about Ruth: happily married, having children, all that her role requires, but still remembered for the act of *hesed* that led her outside the role society expected of her.

The story of Ruth and the story of role distance are still important today because we all risk being lost in our roles, and there are still gender roles. If women and men are lost in their roles they will never connect. We are all the sum of our choices, not our roles. What makes the story of Ruth and Boaz such a great love story is their ability to see past gender stereotypes and discover the human in each other. The reduction of people to the 'other' is as dangerous today as it was then. For the Christian community, there can be no 'others' among us: 'There is no longer Jew or Greek, there is no longer slave or free, there is no longer male and female; for all of you are one in Christ Jesus' (Gal. 3.28). This is what it means for us to be the Church;

this is the kind of view of humanity we are called to model –
there is no 'them', there is only 'us'.

For reflection

- The story of Ruth is often identified as an 'F' voice story,
  perhaps even written by a woman. What can you see in the
  story that might suggest it? Could a man have written the
  book of Ruth?
- Does the book of Ruth question male authority or merely
  work within it?
- It is easy to miss the courage of people on the small stage. The
  courage to stay with someone who needs you, the courage
  to face down prejudice, the courage to do the unexpected.
  But the story of Ruth shows us that such small-stage acts
  show the very quality of God himself. What are the small
  stage acts that show the quality of God in your church?

3

Sarah: made monstrous

Genesis 12—23

A sentence stuck in my mind from one of my favourite television dramas. A man had just murdered the surgeon who put his daughter into a coma by cutting corners with procedures. The victim's son called the murderer 'monstrous'. It was the detective's response that struck me. He replied that if indeed the murderer was monstrous, in this particular case he was '*made* monstrous'.[1]

The story of Sarah, first wife of Abraham, is a puzzling one. She is held up as an example for Jewish and Christian women to follow (1 Pet. 3.6), yet even the most inattentive reading of her story does not seem to make Sarah a role model – she seems rather to be monstrous. She is unbelieving (Gen. 18.12), lies to an angel (Gen. 18.15), bullies her servant Hagar whose body she uses, and eventually, through her jealousy, is responsible for a woman and a child being driven into the desert (Gen. 21.10). Sarah is not, at first sight anyway, a sympathetic character. Phyllis Trible wrote a stimulating article that suggested two ways to read this story. The first was a traditional reading about Abraham and God and faith. The second was that Sarah is written the way she is because her story was written with a patriarchal agenda.[2] Trible argues that in this way of reading, Abraham is given the opportunity to develop a healthy love for his son. He can do this because he is willing to put his God first and therefore learns to love his son in a 'non-attached' way; that is, loving the child for love's sake rather than to satisfy a need within himself. This is a way to understand the sacrifice of Isaac. Sarah, on the other hand, has only her bitterness, her

36

jealousy and her obsessive love for her son. It is not true, Trible argues, to say that Abraham is sacrificing his son, his only son, since there is Ishmael. Isaac is, Trible notes, Sarah's only son, yet she is not given the opportunity to demonstrate faith, to resolve her obsessive love, to be well. Her desire to have a child drove her to mistreat Hagar; her jealous love for Isaac made her force Hagar and Ishmael to leave – we will return to their story in Chapter 9. The bitter words of Sarah that expel Hagar and Ishmael for ever from the family are the last words we hear Sarah utter. Sarah's story 'attributes to her no action or word that might temper her affliction. Instead, it leaves her a jealous and selfish woman.'[3]

However, I wonder whether the writer of Sarah's story might be making another point. It is undeniable that Sarah is a monstrous character and that she is not redeemed or reformed by the end of her story. She is indeed an abusive, bitter bully. Even the writer of 1 Peter can only praise her for, essentially, submitting to oppression – 'Thus Sarah obeyed Abraham and called him lord' (3.6). Power is at the forefront of Sarah's life experience. But at another level the author seems to be doing something else. I argue this because the experience of reading Sarah's story, while it appals us, also leaves us feeling pity for her. This chapter will explore the story to see how the author shows us that a person can indeed be *made monstrous*.

Take your wife

In all her life, at any rate the life within the text, Sarah has known nothing but male power and women as a commodity to be traded. The first thing we hear about Sarah – or Sarai as she then is – is that she has no children and is infertile (Gen. 11.30). This sentence shows us two things: Sarai has not been able to conceive a child herself, and has not, up until now, either adopted a child or used the surrogacy option. The efforts the writer takes to show us that there really are no children in

Abram's bloodline sets up the miraculous nature of the promise that will follow (Gen. 12.1–3). All of the things the Lord
promises Abram really are impossible at this stage: his wife
is infertile (no great nation), a land (already occupied), a great
name (how can an obscure nomad have a great name?).
Nevertheless Abram follows the Lord's command to leave his
home country, takes all his family and belongings and goes.
He trusts God, but the very next episode shows that he trusts
God only up to a point. Wandering into Egypt he forgets the
Lord's promise of blessing and protection and becomes nervous
about his safety. His fears are based on the idea that Sarai
is such a beautiful woman that someone is sure to desire
her and kill him so as to marry her. And he does not spare
Sarai's feelings: he reproaches her for her beauty, which he
was presumably rather glad about before. But now her beauty
is a source of danger to him (Gen. 12.11–12). So from his point
of view Sarai has now 'failed' him in two ways: she has not
given him any children and her gratuitous physical attributes
are going to put him into danger. This way of a certain type
of patriarchal man expressing his sexual fears in terms of
women's attractiveness is not too far from the patriarchal view
even in our time that women who dress in a certain way and who
are victims of sexual violence 'ask for it'. We will come back
to the issue of rape in the Old Testament in a later chapter,
but what should be noted here is that Abram is blaming Sarai
for his danger. His response to danger is to use the source of
danger to protect himself: he uses his wife's body to gain favour
with another man. This actually happens twice (Gen. 12.10–20;
20.1–18). The first time, Pharaoh marries Sarai and apparently has sex with her. The second time, Abimelech takes her
into his harem but has not yet had sex with her when God
intervenes. Each time the text has the word 'take' over and over
again, reflecting Sarai's experience: Abram 'took' Sarai to Egypt
(Gen. 12.5); Sarai 'was taken' into Pharaoh's house (Gen. 12.15);
Abimelech 'takes' her (Gen. 20.2). She has become an object to

be taken, handed over and handed back at the whim of a man. Here, for example, is Pharaoh's reaction when he finds out Sarai is already married: 'Why did you say, "She is my sister", so that I took her for my wife? Now then, here is your wife; *take* her, and be gone' (Gen. 12.19). Abimelech at least offers Sarah the courtesy of speech: he pays over a large sum of money that he calls her vindication (Gen. 20.16). In both episodes we hear the voices of the men involved but never the voice of Sarai, except indirectly in one place where she has dutifully repeated her husband's lie. She may have colluded in the deceit but she has very little choice, as we shall see below. We did not hear her coming out of Ur either. Sarai, the possession to be given and taken, has no voice.

There are two ways of understanding the silencing of Sarai at this point. First, it could be because the author wants Sarai to be silenced as this is a story about Abram. When all is said and done it is his line that will go on – the promise is made to him, after all. Even the explicit promise of a son by Sarai will be made to Abram while Sarai is safely in the tent (Gen. 18.9–10). Or second, it could be that Sarai is silenced because her silence allows the author to make a more complicated point. From the moment Abram decides he will not choose to stand his ground as her husband, Sarai's fate is decided: she will be 'taken' by another man. It will either happen because she follows Abram's plan – which makes her an adulterer – or because she refuses to collude with his deceit and in that case he will be killed. He has taken some trouble to show her that if this happens it will be all her fault for being so beautiful. In that case she would presumably then be 'taken' by her husband's killer. So her choice of whether or not to collude in the concealment only changes what will happen to Abram, not to her. Abram's cowardice has taken the power of protecting her sexual self from her. Her silence indicates an utter powerlessness – the definition of a no-win scenario for Sarai. This is how the author begins to build Sarai's character and motivations. Her experience is that women have no choices and no say – their bodies are for the convenience of men.

It is hard to see what outcome Abram could have envisaged for this deceit except the permanent loss of Sarai. He could not hope to get her back from Pharaoh or Abimelech, after all. Maybe, as David Gunn and Danna Fewell note, Abram just assumes that Sarah is not integral to the promise of descendants – he does not seem to tell her about it until she hears it indirectly from an angel. Perhaps then, in Abram's view, he bears the promise, she is expendable

> if he is giving any thought at all to God's promise that *he* will be a great nation, that *he* will be blessed, that *his* name will be great, that *his* descendants will have land, he is probably of the opinion that a barren wife is hardly going to be any help. He can always find another woman, a younger, fertile woman, preferably . . .[4]

As we will see, the tension between the view of Abram as the only bearer of the promise and God's plan that Sarai should bear the child of promise will lead to serious consequences.

Sakenfeld interprets Sarai's place in this story as being an example of the quality *hesed* that we explored with Ruth.[5] In the second pandering episode, Abraham speaks. When Pharaoh reproached him he said nothing and left, but this time he attempts to justify himself in front of Abimelech, arguing that he thought he had come to a place that had 'no fear of God' and therefore someone would kill him for his wife (Gen. 20.11). He describes to Abimelech the conversation he had with Sarah and recalls asking her to show him this *hesed* of saying to anyone who asks that he is her brother (Gen. 20.13). Sakenfeld argues that *hesed* is essentially a loyalty that has the cost of threatening the one who offers it. Although this interpretation ennobles Sarah, who sacrifices herself for her husband, it has the added dimension of making her an adulterer – one of the worst sins a person can commit in those times.

In exercising this *hesed*, Sarai is put under huge threat. If Pharaoh or Abimelech finds out, either may turn on her. The fact that both these men choose an honourable way out of the issue merely points up how their actions are more righteous than those of Abraham. But when the episode starts there is no guarantee they will act this way. Indeed, Abraham thinks he is sending his wife among people who have no fear of God, as we saw. A much simpler solution from Pharaoh's – or Abimelech's – point of view might have been to have both Sarah and Abraham quietly executed. There is also the risk that the Lord may punish Sarah for consenting to Abraham's plan that makes her an adulterer. The gravity of adultery and the religious fear that surrounded it is clearly shown in the horrified reaction of Pharaoh (Gen. 12.18) and the dream sent to Abimelech (Gen. 20.3–4).

If Sarah has offered Abraham *hesed*, the problem is that in the final analysis it was because he would not offer it to her – he would not risk his life to protect his wife's honour. The second time Sarah is pandered she has heard the promise of children as involving herself (Gen. 18.10). Yet still it seems that Abraham has not taken on board the degree to which Sarah has her role to play: he is still willing to part with her.

Take my slave-girl

We have seen that all Sarai knows is women used as commodities, without much of a say in how they are used, even in how their bodies are used. Small wonder that this abused woman, where she has a little power, abuses it. That is all she knows. And so begins the most appalling story of her actions: the fate of Hagar and Ishmael. In broad outline, Sarai, hearing God's promises but distrusting the miraculous nature of what is offered, decides to bring it about by human means. She uses Hagar, her personal slave, as a surrogate to provide herself with a child. Hagar's story is discussed in more detail in Chapter 9.

What is puzzling in our story is why this option of surrogacy through slave has not been done before. At any rate, up until the promise Abraham and Sarah have apparently been regretfully resigned to having no children – it is almost as if the promise given to Abraham stirs up all the old anxieties long dead. Although to us the idea of using another woman as a womb seems morally repellent, it would not have seemed that way to Sarah's contemporaries – rather, a sensible solution to a serious problem.

From the perspective of her culture, in using another woman as a surrogate mother Sarai has not done anything monstrous. But by putting this event between the experiences of being 'taken' by Pharaoh and 'taken' by Abimelech, the author has set up a terrible irony: surely Sarai should be the very last person to 'take' another woman and give her to a man without a voice? But this is exactly what she does, using exactly the same words: 'So, after Abram had lived for ten years in the land of Canaan, Sarai, Abram's wife, *took* Hagar the Egyptian, her slave-girl, and *gave* her to her husband Abram as a wife' (Gen. 16.3). Hagar is lower down the power structure than Sarai, just as Sarai is lower down it than Abram. Sarai is upholding the very patriarchy that has misused her. There is no empathy in Sarai for Hagar as another victim of male power, no sisterhood. Sarai is colluding in the structures she knows: she never uses Hagar's name, only calls her 'my slave-girl', as we will see in Chapter 9. Even more than that, although the surrogacy was her choice, her description of Hagar's pregnancy can be understood as a 'violence' (Gen. 16.5, although NRSV translates it as 'the wrong'), because it has upset the pecking order: the fertile servant despises the infertile mistress. Sarai even evokes God as a judge between her and her husband. The fury of her speech and the irrational accusation show her emotional state: this was what she wanted, but the reality is hard to bear.

The same ancient laws that provide for a mistress to give her slave as surrogate mother also provide that if the slave despises her mistress she can be punished. In Sarai's case she 'dealt harshly' with Hagar (Gen. 16.6). This word is the same one used to describe the experience of the Hebrews in Egypt (Deut. 26.6). Hagar runs away but is persuaded to return (see Chapter 9). When the child comes, the idea was that he should become Sarai's son, but it all goes wrong. The child is born but somehow Sarai cannot bring herself to love Ishmael (ironically, 'God hears') as her own, and he stays Hagar's son. We get a hint in the fact that Abram names Ishmael and that the author says that Hagar bore him Ishmael – 'Hagar bore Abram a son; and Abram named his son, whom Hagar bore, Ishmael' (Gen. 16.15). This is how Ishmael is remembered, not by his surrogate mother but by his birth mother.

> Abram has held another woman in his arms, and it was Sarah's idea, but she hates it, and she hates her, and she hates him, and she hates their soon-to-be child, and she hates herself, and she probably hates the God who closed her own womb.[6]

Taken

Time wears on. God appears to Abram and renames both him and Sarai, who becomes Sarah, and underlines for him that Sarah is the wife who will bear the chosen son (Gen. 17.15–16). Abraham snorts. Abraham knows that in the natural order of things neither he nor Sarah are capable of having children. So he offers God Ishmael, already extant (Gen. 17.17–18). He still does not understand that Sarah has a place in God's plan – in his thinking, as Gunn and Fewell noted above, any woman will do. God insists: he will find a place for Ishmael but the son of the promise must be Sarah's son.

Later three messengers appear to tell the news to Abraham again and to Sarah this time. Sarah reacts exactly as Abraham has: a snort of derisive laughter. She feels she is 'worn out' and he is old – maybe they are not even sexually functional any more. Sarah asks if she will have 'pleasure' (Gen. 18.12) – a clear irony here as the word for pleasure, *edenah*, echoes Eden, the place of fertility.[7] But is there more than just disbelief in Sarah's reaction? Gerald Janzen argues that this promise causes fear because it undermines the settled order of their lives.[8] The text does not tell us anything more than the fact that Sarah believes what she is being promised is biologically impossible, but Janzen's idea fits psychologically. Sarah's life, at least as far as the text tells us, has been painful. She has been used and abused, she has used and been abusive. God, it seems, wants to challenge her perception of hopelessness, and the three address her, even though indirectly, reminding her that nothing is too wonderful for the Lord (Gen. 18.14).

When the messengers told Sarah she was going to have a child she laughed in disbelief; when Isaac is born she laughs again, this time in joy. Not only that, she says that everyone who hears about this miraculous child will laugh too:

> Now the laughter becomes a different kind of disbelief as when one disbelieves for joy ... at something too good to be true ... For the moment, Sarah's soul opens to embrace all who will laugh with her.[9]

But it does not last. Once she has a biological son of her own, whatever feelings she may have had towards Ishmael erupt into a ferocious jealousy. There has been great discussion about exactly what the young Ishmael was doing that provoked Sarah's words and actions. The Hebrew says he was laughing ('Isaacing') and the Greek adds 'with Isaac'. It may be that the deliberate use of the word suggests that Ishmael is trying to supplant his little brother by being Isaac with Isaac, or possibly that he is mocking the child (as his mother once treated Sarai with contempt), or that he was simply laughing with Isaac. The ambiguity of what Ishmael was doing is echoed in NRSV's translation of 'playing with', which can be a positive or a negative thing. There is a lot of laughter in these stories, some of it joyful, some of it very bitter. Ishmael's laughter, whether he was mocking or playing, costs him dearly.

Quite often Christian commentators want to interpret Ishmael's actions as mocking Isaac, thus putting him under the curse of those who treat Abram's family with contempt (Gen. 12.3). They do this because they are keen to excuse Abraham – as he now is – and God for the sending away of a woman and a boy into the desert. In this argument Sarah is doing what is right by righting the contempt shown to the family: she is merely enacting the warning in the Abrahamic blessing. But Abraham does not seem to see the sending away as justice. The text does not make it clear how we are to understand what Ishmael did. I suggest it is more plausible to the character of Sarah to interpret her actions in the light of her feelings. Janzen reflects on Sarah's possible motives: she may not trust God enough – like Abraham in the past when he pimped her; she may see the boy an 'alien threat'; she might think she is acting alongside God to secure the promise.[10] It may be that there is a little of all of this. What we can say is that Sarah has managed to achieve the reverse of *hesed*: she can sacrifice two vulnerable members of her household for her son's safety, just as she was once sacrificed for Abraham's. This kind of use of people is all she has known.

The last words we ever hear Sarah say are these: 'Cast out this slave woman with her son; for the son of this slave woman shall not inherit along with my son Isaac' (Gen. 21.10). Sarah has broken faith with custom, with Hagar, with Ishmael. She still cannot trust God for his promises: she must eliminate any threat to Isaac. Jealousy and distrust are the characteristics she shows at this point in the story. As this is the last we hear her say, it is how we remember her. As Trible says: 'This utterance haunts Sarah's portrait, crying out for release from possessiveness and attachment.'[11]

The story does indeed not allow Sarah healing. Trible argues that if *Sarah* had been allowed to go up the mountain with

Isaac, she could have experienced the healing Abraham found there – she could have been freed from her corrosive possessiveness, which Trible calls 'attachment'. But if the story has denied her resolution, it has at least offered the reader something else: an explanation for how she acts and a reason to pity her. Sarah has acted in ways that we find both morally and emotionally repellent. She is monstrous. But she is also herself a victim and therefore cannot be dismissed as not worthy of our empathy. Her story is told in such a way as to make it clear that Sarah is what she has been made. Trible argues that the author and patriarchy have led to a portrait of Sarah as bitter and selfish. I want to add to this a little in the light of the effect that Sarah's story has on me as reader. The author's description of patriarchy and its abuses shows how a woman can be made both monstrous and pitiful. In this reading I believe the author is criticizing what has happened to Sarah. In her early days she showed *hesed* but her life experience has driven it from her.

Why does the story of Sarah still matter? First, because it reminds us that oppression casts a long shadow. Second, because the most important thing to be done in a case of oppression is to stop the oppression and help victims heal, help them recover their sense of self-worth. But the second most important thing to do is surely to help the oppressors change, and this requires that we see them as people and not just oppressors. Sometimes, although not always, the oppression is part of a cycle oppressors have known, and may have gone on for generations: they may themselves be victims as well as perpetrators. This is not to minimize the sinfulness of the oppression, for everyone has a choice to make about how they repeat what they have experienced. However, the love of God can break the cycle and allow release. Sarah never had the opportunity – at least in the text – for this kind of healing and change, but her story tells us clearly why it is so important.

For reflection

- Is reading Sarah as victim as well as bully what the author intended?
- How does understanding Sarai's actions as *hesed* in the early episode add to the story?
- Is Sarah denied the chance to heal by the author's choice?
- How has the Church been oppressor in its time and how can we avoid repeating those mistakes?

Part 2

WOMEN AND MEN

4

The Levite's concubine: petrified of silence?

Judges 19—21

This chapter focuses on silence. The reason is to ask questions about the truly horrible story of Judges 19—21. This story, as perhaps nowhere else in the Old Testament except 2 Samuel 13, which we will also consider briefly, shows how easily men can abuse their power over women in a patriarchal society.

The story begins, apparently, as an episode in a love story. A concubine leaves her man. Neither of them is named, and it is even difficult to find the right English terms for their relationship. Concubinage in Israel was a respectable state – a socially recognized sexual relationship not unlike, but not the same as, marriage. It must be said, though, that a concubine had less status than a wife. The man is referred to as a 'man' – which is the same word as husband – and also as 'her lord', as well as 'Levite'. The woman is referred to as 'concubine' but also as 'woman', which can also mean 'wife'. In this chapter I will simply use 'woman' because I do not want to define her by her sexual relationship but by her personhood.

After the woman has gone the Levite decides he wants her back and so goes to her father's house to find her. But once there he spends his time drinking and feasting with his father-in-law and does not seem to notice the concubine at all. Nevertheless she goes home with him. They find themselves benighted and the Levite consults with his (male) servant and decides to try and get to Gibeah or Ramah, avoiding Jerusalem because at this stage it is not an Israelite town. In view of what will happen in an Israelite town, his xenophobia has a horrible irony about it – they might have done better among the Canaanites. When they reach Gibeah they are advised not to spend the night in the town square and are taken in by an old man. Clearly Gibeah is a dangerous place. The men of Gibeah try to force the old man to make the Levite come out so they can rape him. Instead the old man offers the angry mob his virgin daughter and the concubine. The outcome is extraordinarily brutal: the woman is pushed out by her own man into the town square and gang-raped all night. The next morning the Levite makes his departure. Finding her dead or dying, he takes her home and cuts her body up into 12 parts as a protest and sends one part of her mutilated body to each of the twelve tribes:

> Then he commanded the men whom he sent, saying, 'Thus shall you say to all the Israelites, "Has such a thing ever happened since the day that the Israelites came up from the land of Egypt until this day? Consider it, take counsel, and speak out."' (Judg. 19.30)

Cutting her body up and spreading the pieces across Israel might be deemed as terrible as the gang-rape, for it denies her the chance for burial – and not to be buried is the worst fate in Israel, as in the case of Jezebel (2 Kings 9.35–37). But the violence does not stop there: the tribes of Israel then begin a war against the men of Gibeah to punish them. The Benjaminites come out for Gibeah, which is in Benjamin. For two days the Benjaminites have the upper hand and 40,000 Israelites die. On the third day Benjamin is defeated and over 25,000 of them die in battle, plus the whole city of Gibeah. Once the fighting has died down the Israelites become concerned for Benjamin as they have sworn never to marry their daughters to a Benjaminite, so there is now a real chance that the tribe of Benjamin might die out. Their solution is to find a town that did not swear the oath: Jabesh-Gilead. Everyone is executed except 400 young women who are virgins, or at least unattached girls of an age to be married. They are sent to Shiloh and married off to the remaining Benjaminites. Any Benjaminite who did not get a wife is encouraged to watch for the girls of Shiloh when they come out to dance at a festival and then perform what is commonly called marriage by rape.

It is an appalling story. If we saw it on the news we would wince in horror and ask why nothing is being done. Yet here it is in our Bible. What on earth are we to do with it? Of course, violence among men and violence against women are not new themes and we see it in many other places. But when Phyllis Trible called this the 'extravagance' of violence[1] she encapsulated its extreme and appalling nature.

Protected and unprotected

Trible begins with the attitude of the men. The Levite is apparently attached to the woman for he makes a long journey to persuade her to return home. His intention as he sets out is to 'speak to her heart' (Judg. 19.3 – Trible's translation, from the Hebrew text's use of the word 'heart'). Perhaps the old English word 'woo' would work for us here. But here the romance ends for, as Trible points out, he does not actually speak to her at all![2] Carousing in the company of his father-in-law is apparently more attractive. Not a word is spoken to or by the woman. From the very moment the Levite re-enters her life to talk to her she is utterly silenced. We have no idea what she thought about her man coming to fetch her and whether she went willingly, because she never speaks. Quite possibly she had no choice and her father pushed her out of the door. We can note here how this silencing, this lack of indication of her feelings, a similar silence to the one we saw when Sarah was pandered in Genesis, sets up the tenor of her story. In the same way, she has no part in the vital decision about where to stay the night.

When they find themselves benighted in Gibeah, the old man might be seen as a rescuer. But he is only interested in rescuing the man: as Trible points out, the rules of hospitality here only extend to the male guest.[3] A woman and a young girl – since girls were probably married once they reached menarche and left home – are apparently an acceptable trade-off. Trible suggests that this is deliberate, for a sexually experienced woman and a virgin girl will appeal to different tastes, and goes further: sexually violating a man is described by the old man as a 'vile thing'. But if it is done to women the old man speaks of it as 'the good in your eyes' – Trible uses this expression to set up a link with the final comment of the author (Judg. 21.25). In this story men must always have their way, 'even wicked ones', and this can be achieved by sacrificing women.[4] The woman is utterly silent throughout her ordeal and it is only when her man comes out in the morning that he finally speaks directly to her. But what speech: he curtly orders her to move. The Hebrew only needs two words: *qumi vnelechah*, 'Get up . . . we are going' (Judg. 19.28). 'Where are the words which speak to her heart? Certainly not here.'[5]

There is also a dreadful possibility that the woman is not even dead at this stage. Perhaps, slung over the donkey, she was carried home dying or comatose. He might have killed her when he took up the knife. Trible observes that the Hebrew text does not use any word that could make her death clear,[6] hence is silent about her death. This is to protect the Levite, who may have actually killed her. Trible suggests that the silencing of the woman indicates that neither the men nor the author recognize the concubine's humanity. The Levite then does his dreadful deed: as Trible observes, the men of Gibeah did theirs by night, his is done in the daylight.[7] As the story progresses, the outcome of this dreadful gang-rape is hundreds more rapes, this time rapes sanctioned by Israel.

Complicit silence?

The idea that in ancient Israel there could be sexually violent men (the men of Gibeah), a fool who would put the safety of a man above that of a woman and even his own little girl (the old man), a callous coward who would hide behind his woman (the Levite) and a nation who answer violence with even more violence, is not surprising even if it is appalling. The issue for readers is the apparent unwillingness of the author to make any kind of explicit judgement on the characters. The question is whether the reader should interpret this to mean the author sees nothing to disapprove of in the Levite's actions and those of the old man. They have, as Trible argued above, used a help-less woman to guarantee the safety of a man. It is possible to interpret this as meaning that the author does not care about the fate of the woman: his view is entirely androcentric. Moreover there are questions to be asked about the role of God in all this. Trible notes that there are some linguistic connections to the story of the sacrifice of Isaac in Genesis 22 – for example, the phrase 'took a/the knife' (Gen. 22.10). Trible draws the contrast that God intervenes to save Isaac when Abraham 'took the knife', speaking to Abraham to prevent the sacrifice. But when the Levite 'took a knife' there is no speech of God to prevent this killing of a woman – God too is silent. Trible argues that the author uses silence to protect the man from accusation. God is silent when speech could have saved, as it did for Isaac.[8]

We expect that the word of God should stand against these actions, not stand back and refuse to condemn them. Many scholars have observed that the author of Judges uses this story as an illustration of what happens when 'there was no king in Israel: all the people did what was right in their own eyes' (Judg. 21.25). Indeed, the author uses this phrase three times towards the end of the book and clearly means us to see that this is how the various dreadful events and the interminable cycle of Israel's unfaithfulness, repentance, rescue and unfaithfulness is propagated in the earlier chapters. Only a king, runs the implication, can keep Israel acting in appropriate, faithful ways. Trible notes all this but observes that a political solution will be ineffectual for there is a certain dreadful irony in the implied belief that a king can regulate the behaviour of his people.[9] Many scholars believe that the final editing of Judges was done during and after the exile by a 'Deuteronomistic' historian. This book forms part of what Martin Noth identified as the 'Deuteronomistic History': a history stretching from the first conquest of the land of Canaan to the fall of Jerusalem.[10] This overall collection of stories has a focus bound up in similar views to the book of Deuteronomy, hence Deuteronomistic History. The books contained in this history are Joshua, Judges, 1 and 2 Samuel, 1 and 2 Kings.

If this idea of the Deuteronomistic History is persuasive – and it certainly has widespread acceptance albeit with various modifications – then the 'historian(s)' did his/their editing and collecting in the time of the exile and after. He/they knew, therefore, that putting a king in place in Israel did not prevent crimes of violence. The house of David will have acts of sexual violence as part of its legacy, including another rape – that of Tamar by her brother Amnon – and this is why Trible observes, as we saw above, that political solutions will not work. In that story (2 Sam. 13) the female victim of the rape is not silent: her anguish and pain are voiced by the author. 'But Tamar put ashes on her head, and tore the long robe that she was wearing; she put her hand on her head, and went away, crying aloud as she went' (2 Sam. 13.19). But in the end Tamar too is silenced, not by the author but by another character in the story, for she is forced to withdraw to her older brother's house and live out her life there, shut away.

> Her brother Absalom said to her, 'Has Amnon your brother been with you? Be quiet for now, my sister; he is your brother; do not take this to heart.' So Tamar remained, a desolate woman, in her brother Absalom's house. (2 Sam. 13.20)[11]

We might also note that Tamar is told to be silent and (literally) 'not set your heart on the matter'. Nobody spoke to the concubine's heart and Absalom denies Tamar the right even to feel the grief, anger and horror about what happened to her. Absalom intends to punish his brother but only the author allows his sister the right to lament.

Often Christians talk about reading stories in the context of the whole Bible – 'the whole counsel of Scripture' as it is called. This is a reliable method: it protects, in theory at least, from proof-texting – taking a unit of text out of its context and allowing it to drive an entire interpretation – and from allowing small things to have an importance they should not, or failing to see the importance of a really significant idea that develops across the whole of the Bible. With regard to this big, vile crime, the whole context has little to say about it explicitly. There are two more references explicitly to the Judges episode in the Old Testament, both in Hosea. The actions of the men of Gibeah are used as an example of what is wrong in Israel: 'deeply corrupted . . . as in the days of Gibeah' (Hos. 9.9) and 'since the days of Gibeah you have sinned' (Hos. 10.9). Trible argues that two references are hardly enough for such an egregious offence. The New Testament similarly is silent and makes no reference to the events – 'Silence covers impotence and complicity.'[12] Trible argues that the canon offers some small comfort in the form of a healing perspective.[13] The next story in the Hebrew Bible is the story of Hannah, who is noted for her worth and her faith, as we shall see. In that story a family, like the Levite, from the hill country of Ephraim will be heard by a gracious deity, and Hannah's son will minister at Shiloh, scene of the rape of 200 girls. In the Greek Bible the next story is that of Ruth who, as we have seen, is what Trible calls a 'study in female hospitality'.[14]

The silence of considering?

Silence may mean complicity or it may mean criticism. If the author does not condemn the male characters, neither has he anything to say about the Levite's retribution being justice.

Instead he observes for the third time in the book that in those days there was no king in Israel and everyone did 'the good in their own eyes'. In this way he subverts and criticizes the words of the old man who so blithely abandoned the woman to her fate, telling the rapists of Gibeah to do 'the good in your eyes'. The author makes the woman silent and nameless, but he certainly tells us a lot about her that is designed to draw the reader's empathy and horror: the pathetic detail that she crawls back and is found dead or dying, clutching the threshold of a house that did not protect her (Judg. 19.27). The description of what happened to her, using two verbs, one to convey having sex and the other to convey abuse, foregrounds the dreadful nature of it – the language is brutal to describe a brutal event. In the same way, her silence emphasizes the reality of her life: she has no choices.

The author does not seem to be explicitly prescriptive in how he tells this story. It may be, though, that he has included the implication of what he thinks. Throughout Judges the author has avoided making judgements on the many extra-ordinary things that happen – a good example might be the life of Samson. But in the case of the story we are considering, it may be that the author has used the words of the Levite himself to pass judgement. For when the Levite sends the parts of the woman's body all over Israel, he tells the Israelites to consider 'this thing' and take counsel, as we saw. But the author makes the speech ambiguous about what 'this thing' is that they need to consider. It might be the gang-rape; it might be the taking of the Levite's property by coercion, for so he seems to have seen the woman. But the reader has a wider scope of 'things' to consider. The reader might pass judgement on his maltreatment of the woman in failing to protect her; his maltreatment of her body by scattering it and denying her burial; or indeed even his possible killing of her. Which of these extravagantly violent acts should the reader 'consider'? Trible notes that 'this thing' is a feminine form in Hebrew and so highlights the woman who is the victim.[15] The Levite seemed confident that the Israelites who got the message would all agree with him, and so it proves. But asking people to consider is a dangerous pastime, for they may just 'consider' what you have done! Instead of stating a crime and the retribution he requires, the author has made the Levite open his acts to the same scrutiny by the reader as the actions of the men of Gibeah. In this way the author of Judges invites his readers to 'consider' and condemn all the violators, fools and cowards.

Trible, as we have seen, compares the experience of the concubine to that of Isaac in the episode where he is nearly sacrificed on the mountain, called in Jewish thought the Akedah ('binding'). But in the Akedah God speaks twice, once to order the sacrifice and once to save Isaac. In our story God does not speak at all. If this is an Akedah, it is a godless one, not ordered by God. It is not only the woman who is silent – God shares her silence. This too may be an indication of the author's view of how God views what has happened.

It is true that God intervenes to save some people from the situation in which they find themselves and not others. He speaks sometimes and is silent sometimes. It is the cry of all who also believe in God in the face of suffering: 'Why didn't you stop it?' It is painful to recognize, but part of the reality of the life of faith. There is not space here to go over the question of innocent suffering and indeed, this side of death, I do not believe there is a full answer – although it is the duty of the Church to hear suffering, remember it and alleviate it in any way we can. But there is a promise of a man on a cross who is also God: the God who has known suffering.

If the woman is silent, her story is not. As I was writing this book, news was breaking of a horrible and extended campaign of sexual abuse by a well-known celebrity, now dead. The man cannot be brought to justice now but some of the victims who were finally able to speak out spoke not only of their frustration but also about the relief that their story would be heard and believed, that this might go some way to helping them heal. The woman in our story was beyond healing, but her story is heard, remembered, read out in churches and synagogues. This story of a rape is foregrounded in the book of Judges. What happens to the woman in all its brutality and the fate of the hapless girls at Shiloh are the horrible climax of the book, bringing to fullness all the violence and immorality the book has already shown in a kingless Israel where the author tells us that self-chosen morality is king. The woman is silent, as the suffering servant of Isaiah 52.13—53.10 is silent, but like him she is centre stage. Her story shouts at the reader, demanding attention. Those who have been silenced, even as the woman was silenced, may find their story shouted here.

For reflection

- Would an author who cared about her fate have voiced the woman?
- Should an author always explicitly condemn an evil act or risk making it seem acceptable by silence?
- How can the Church learn to hear stories in a way to help the abused?

5

The woman of Shunem:
independent woman?

2 Kings 4.8–37; 8.1–6

The story of the woman of Shunem is one of the rare stories where a woman acts largely independently of her man. It has several episodes. As her story begins, Elisha is making visits to Shunem and the woman decides to set him up a guest room in her house. Wanting to make some return for her hospitality he offers to help her with local authorities. When she refuses he promises her a son, and despite her incredulity the son arrives. Later the child is working in the field with his father and dies, perhaps of sunstroke. The woman goes to Elisha and pleads for his help and the prophet brings the child back to life. Later still, on Elisha's advice the woman and her family flee a famine in the area. When she returns she goes to the king to get her land back. Elisha's servant Gehazi happens to be there and he tells the king about the miracle child. The king assigns an official and the woman's land is given back to her.

The contrast in the two stories in chapter 4 could not be greater. In 2 Kings 4.1–7 Elisha comes to the aid of another destitute widow, but in this first story the widow appeals for Elisha's help and does it on the basis of a prior claim: her husband was one of the 'company of the prophets', possibly the support staff who went with the prophet. She is entirely dependent for everything on Elisha's help or she will starve. She has a son but no means of support. Her community is a source of threat for she has a creditor who wants to take her children as debt-slaves. The woman of Shunem, on the other hand, is perhaps one of the most independent women we see in the Old Testament. She is married, naturally: singleness in a woman apart from widowhood is largely unknown in the Old Testament. But her husband is not a fully drawn character: he is one-dimensional and his main purpose is to contrast with her, as we shall see. He intervenes in the narrative only to ask foolish questions that serve to highlight the woman's theological surefootedness. She has means, evidently, but no child. She apparently stands well in her community and does not need anything – indeed, she turns down Elisha's offer of help. We can see her quality of independent thinking at the beginning of her story – it is she who has the spiritual awareness to recognize Elisha's quality as a prophet (2 Kings 4.9). She makes Elisha a room in the house. Although she says 'Let us' to her husband, his reply is not included: it seems his approval is not really important.

Patron and protégé

Elisha recognizes that her hospitality is beyond the norm and so offers the woman – not her husband – a favour. This has immense importance for us: the prophet does not send for the head of the household but the person who has been actively concerned with him. Elisha does not address the woman directly but has Gehazi, his servant, speak to her. Many feminist scholars have identified this, along with Elisha's calling her, as the Hebrew has it literally, 'this Shunemmite' (2 Kings 4.12), as a sign that he wishes to maintain distance or even express contempt for the woman. If this is so, the author at any rate does not seem to share his contempt: from him she receives the title 'great woman', again as the Hebrew says literally (2 Kings 4.8). I do not think it is a question of contempt so much as Elisha's anxiety about power, as we will see. Elisha is uncomfortable because he is in the position of protégé to patron, as is indicated by his repeated attempts to repay her hospitality and the ways he speaks about her in Shunem. What follows is a series of utterances designed to realign who is patron and who is protégé.

Belonging

Elisha tells Gehazi to ask the woman if she would like him to use his authority to gain favour with the powers that be in her area (2 Kings 4.13). She apparently seeks no favours and responds proudly to Gehazi: 'I live among my own people'. The woman's first reply to Elisha's first offer is that she does not need any help. She could have asked the miracle-working prophet to give her a son but she does not. Tirka Frymer-Kensky argues that her reply shows that women with wealth are less anxious about their own childlessness.

> The same economic security makes it possible for her to enjoy both status and a secure old age even without ever having had a child. The story of the Shunnemite can be understood as a biblical example of how women act when the *economic* constraints of patriarchy are removed.[1]

This is no doubt true but her reply also offers another perspective: it constitutes a refusal of Elisha's patronage. It establishes distance and belonging, even as he has been attempting to do. He distanced her by speaking to her indirectly and referring to her by a marker that made her different from him and foreign ('this Shunemmite'). She first demolishes the distance between them that he created, by speaking directly to him. Then she establishes a distance of her own making. Her statement that she lives among *her own* people reminds him that foreignness is a matter of perspective. The woman has apparently a complex web of support networks of which she is part and upon which she can call at need. She turns the tables on Elisha by excluding him from this network. He is the visiting preacher not the home-grown prophet – he is only passing through; she belongs.

She is indeed 'this Shunemmite' and as such she needs no help from the Abel-Meholahite (Elisha). Elisha's attempted reversal has failed. Her sense of belonging in her community counters his intention to make her dependent on him.

What every woman wants?

Elisha, in his desire to 'do something for her', turns to Gehazi for insight, and here is one of the most puzzling aspects from a purely informational point of view. If Gehazi knows she has no child, surely Elisha, who lived in the house, knows it as well. Claudia Camp notes that the Shunemmite is unusual in that her childlessness is not revealed from the beginning of the story: usually childlessness is introduced early on into a character's description, as for example in Genesis 11.30. Camp suggests that the woman therefore has 'an authority independent of mother-hood'.[2] It is true that having children was seen as integral to a woman's life because it was so vital to the well-being of the family. Children were nothing more or less than survival. Economically they guaranteed a means of producing food when the parents were too old to go out into the fields. But more than that, in the thought-world of the Old Testament having children was a form of continuance that was the extent of their ideas of immortality: the name – of the man, naturally – would go down the generations and therefore he would not be entirely forgotten in Sheol.

If we continue to observe power relationships in the conversation, the reason for Elisha's question becomes clearer. Gehazi voices a need that the woman will not – thus a kindness can be done for her without compromising her piety. Were she simply to accept the favour she could be understood as offering hospitality on a quid pro quo basis. The author is apparently anxious that the reader should not misconstrue her pious hospitality towards the prophet. We are not told if she is still of an age to bear children but it is said that her husband is old

– the implication being, no longer capable of having sex. This is possibly the only place in the Old Testament where childlessness is attributed to the man and not the woman.

There is a darker side to this exchange between Elisha and Gehazi, however. The conversation begins by distancing the woman even more firmly. Elisha speaks to Gehazi and Gehazi replies – the woman is not even present. In this dialogue where the decision is made to grant her a child, the woman has been entirely removed from the decision-making process: 'done for' will become 'done to'. Fokkelien van Dijk-Hemmes comments that the miraculous child being unasked for indicates to us the patriarchal outlook of the text, which cannot tolerate a woman who might choose to be childless.[3] We might note that the husband does not get any say either. I suggest, however, that what is important here is the nature of what is offered: it is the one thing that the woman cannot do for herself. Elisha's search to make himself patron moves from something she already has to something she can never have without his miraculous intervention. The use of third-person-singular 'she has no son' (2 Kings 4.14) at this point brackets the husband out even more than the wife.

When he was dealing with a completely vulnerable and helpless widow, Elisha felt secure enough to involve her in the process (2 Kings 4.2), asking her in person how he could help. It is true that he then immediately told her what to do but the question has rhetorical importance as establishing her as part of the conversation. Here, however, made insecure by someone who has helped him rather than the other way round, he will not ask her or even speak directly to her. Then, once he is satisfied that he has found a way to put the woman into the position of a protégée, Elisha is willing to address her directly and announces the birth of a son at the same time of year. The woman's reply is an attack, not on what he offers but on his reliability: she reuses the title she gave him at the beginning of the episode, here as an intentional irony – to rebuke the 'man of God' who is returning her generosity with a lie (2 Kings 4.16). But Elisha is proved right when the child is born. Moreover the author apparently sides with Elisha by the use of the reiterative 'as Elisha had declared to her' (2 Kings 4.17), implying a rebuke to her lack of faith in Elisha. We do not know whether the Shunemmite did or did not want a child. What is indicated is that she did not believe it could – or perhaps should – happen. Her reaction indicates resistance but it is not entirely clear to what. It may be to the improbability of the miracle and perhaps to Elisha's insistence on making himself the patron and her the protégée. This is underscored by the later reproach when the child dies. The Shunemmite woman accuses Elisha of deceiving her and insisting on giving her a gift when she had asked for nothing (2 Kings 4.28).

Thinking independently

When the child comes we are not told explicitly how the Shunemmite woman felt about him, but we get an idea of the kind of mother she is by the desperate and poignant picture of her cradling the miracle child to her bosom as he dies slowly (2 Kings 4.20). The actions of the father function to sharpen that picture by contrasting with it. He commands the servant to take the child 'to his mother' – the father does not carry the child in himself but gets a servant to do it (2 Kings 4.19). He is effectively distanced from care for the child in the same way as he was from the decision to welcome the prophet and from the prophecy that promised the child in the first place. After the child has died, the husband's main concern is protocol: one may not make extraordinary visits to prophets, only at the appropriate time (2 Kings 4.23). The husband is portrayed as a foolish, indifferent man; the woman is able, even in this crisis, to think more clearly. The couple recall Manoah and his wife. In that story the future mother of Samson is visited by an angel to announce the promise of Samson. When she tells Manoah he does not believe her until the angel visits him personally – then he reacts in fear because they have seen God and he thinks therefore they will die (Judg. 13.22–23). His wife, whose name we never learn, observes that there would not be much point in the angel announcing a pregnancy if he meant to kill them. This kind of reasoned theology is much the same as the Shunemmite is able to command: she knows it will be all right in these desperate circumstances to bother the prophet (2 Kings 4.23).

The Shunemmite does not allow her husband to talk her out of her quest. The next barrier between her and the prophet is Gehazi, sent by Elisha to make enquiries – it may be that Elisha is again trying to keep her at a distance. She politely brushes Gehazi's enquiries to one side, heading straight for the prophet himself. Even when she manages to speak to Elisha he does not want to come himself but tries to send Gehazi on his behalf to perform the miracle. The Shunemmite will not accept that either and stays with him until he comes himself – again she refuses to accept the male power structure. She apparently intends that events unfold the way she thinks they should. But there is more than highhandedness in this. Perhaps also, since it was Gehazi who suggested she could be given a son, she is anxious to make it clear that she does not consider him in any way her benefactor.

But the way she speaks to the prophet is surprising also, and perhaps this is the main reason for her not dealing with Gehazi. By speaking to him directly she asks for his help but only implicitly; what she does explicitly is question and reproach: 'Did I ask my lord for a son? Did I not say, Do not mislead me?' (2 Kings 4.28). Again the word for deceiving crosses her lips, as it did when Elisha promised her a son – it is a grave accusation to make against a prophet. By Elisha prophesying this child and the Lord taking him, she is now worse off than she was before. Her anguish at the death of her son is deepened by her indignation at this prophet who interferes in people's lives, giving them things they never asked for and making every-thing worse in the process. Her insistence that Elisha deal with the disaster is again almost that of a patron with a well-meaning but thoughtless protégé.

The importance of her speech to the story is indicated by the fact that the prophet of the Lord has no idea what has gone wrong when she first comes. This allows space in the logic of the narrative for her fully to articulate not only what has happened but her feelings about it. That the author has created this space indicates the importance he attached to her speech. Johanna van Wijk-Bos argues that this expression of pain is vital for women: 'Women have been robbed of the power to name; it is an essential step for us to find words for our experience.'[4] Indeed, it is vital for everyone but, building on Van Wijk-Bos's argument, women are traditionally voiced much less in patriarchal societies. Not in this story, though: the full range of her grief and rage spill out in front of Elisha.

Elisha is eventually able to bring the little boy back to life. This final miracle gets no proud response – some favours can only be accepted. The last we see of the woman in this episode is as she bows before Elisha and then takes her son. The story then could be interpreted overall as a sort of taming of the shrew episode. Does the author want to show an independent woman tamed by the fears and cares of childrearing, returning to her proper place? An answer is provided in the third episode of her story.

The taming of the Shunemmite?

The overwhelming picture we have of the Shunemmite up until her son is revived is of a woman who is independent, warm-hearted, intelligent and sassy, pious and generous. From this point onwards she seems to become a more traditional woman: grateful, submissive. There is a third episode where Elisha again intervenes to help her household, in which his advice enables her to avoid a famine (2 Kings 8.1–6). This time there is no assertion that she is secure in her own community. Returning at the end of the famine, she needs to appeal to the king for the return of her property – such things happen in times of turmoil. It seems reasonable to assume that the husband is dead since the woman now has to appeal to the king. The son is either not of an age to take his place as the head of the household or is no longer in her life for whatever reason. The structure of her society means that inevitably the Shunemmite is going to need to appeal to a man for what she needs. Thus women are always, in such a society, dependent by the fact of their gender.[5] The Old Testament does not explicitly challenge this structure – at best it seeks to improve and safeguard the lot of dependants. The Shunemmite is now not so far from the widow of 2 Kings 4.1–7. Such is the fate of women the world over in patriarchal societies. And in this episode, it is again Elisha who affects her destiny, at least at the beginning.

However, this final episode where we meet the Shunemmite has some interesting undercurrents. As many feminist scholars have pointed out, once the mother of a miracle child has had the child, she ceases to become a major character in the story.[6] But when we meet the Shunemmite for the second time she is still active, still running the household, still looking out for her family. It is yet again Gehazi who is the intermediary but in this scene it is Elisha who is being spoken about, not spoken to – he does not figure in the episode in the court. Mark Roncace paints a humorous picture by observing that the tenses in the Hebrew indicate that the woman arrives just as Gehazi is telling his stories and she interrupts him.[7] Again we see the Shunemmite reversing the power balance: she does not allow Gehazi to speak for her. As she did with Elisha, she goes straight to the top. Gehazi introduces her as the woman whose son was restored to life. He does not mention her current state of destitution, which might have been more to the point. The king then asks the woman about her situation and the woman speaks directly to the king to explain her needs. The king then appoints an official who makes sure her property is restored to her. In the end Elisha's first offer, to speak to the king for her, comes to nothing. As Roncace observes, the woman herself approaches the king and the king acts for her through his official.[8] In a final twist of irony, the person who actively restores the Shunemmite's property to her is a eunuch: a completely childless man. At the beginning of the story a childless woman is given a child but he is too young to help her when she needs him: she is saved by her own intervention with the king and a childless man. 'While she was happily living among her own people, it turns out that if she did need a word with the king, she was quite capable of acquiring it.'[9]

Elisha, the author and the king all refer to the house and land as 'hers'. In strict understanding of Israelite law, of course, it is not hers but her son's. But by referring to the house and land this way it is clear that the woman from Shunem is still very much the household decision-maker. It may be that the son is still too young to take on the burden of the head of the household, so the Shunemmite woman fulfils this role until he can. This is the reality of an Israelite woman's life: she only has authority if there is no man available. But within the limits of her society the Shunemmite is indeed an independent woman. Her life is lived out in patriarchy, but she is not an androcentric character – she is the 'great woman' (2 Kings 4.8), as the Hebrew text describes her.

Independence of thought and action are vital to human freedom. They must, of course, be counterbalanced by the needs and rights of others – the 'greater good'. In a patriarchal society many will believe that male authority is the greater good, for men and for women, for domestic and societal harmony. Sometimes it is even argued that women should not do certain things because they simply do not have the same capacity for them as men. The story of the woman of Shunem, making good decisions and acting as a source of wellbeing as head of her household, allows us to challenge all these views.

For reflection

- What role does the Shunemmite's husband play?
- Some scholars say that Elisha is being critiqued in this story. Do you agree, and what in the story makes you think so?
- To what extent is the Shunemmite really independent?
- How do Christians express criticism in a Christlike way?

6

Michal: the thin line between love and hate

1 Samuel 18—19; 2 Samuel 3.13–16; 6.12–23

Michal is the daughter of King Saul, first king of Israel. She falls in love with the young, handsome man, David, who has been brought to her father's court. When she is married to him her father's jealousy of his son-in-law increases and Michal shows heroic determination in helping him escape from her father's jealousy. She puts a dummy in their bed when her father's guards come looking for David and enables him to escape. David is forced to hide out for a long time. Later she is married off to another man, whether by consent or not the text does not tell us. When David returns he reclaims Michal as his wife and brings her to his palace. But this love story – if that is what it is – ends badly. 'And Michal the daughter of Saul had no child to the day of her death' (2 Sam. 6.23) – so ends a story that is, outside of the stories of sexual violence, possibly one of the most tragic in the Old Testament.

It ends an episode that should have been one only of joy – that of the ark's arrival in Jerusalem (2 Sam. 6). David strips to his underwear and dances with joy before the ark, safely arrived in the king's city, sign of the presence, power and favour of the Lord himself – no wonder he danced. And then he went home, the acclamations of his people still ringing in his ears, to 'bless his household' (2 Sam. 6.20). It is not hard to imagine what that blessing might consist in as far as his wife is concerned as he runs indoors towards her, endorphins rushing in his veins. And his reception is a blistering stream of contempt: 'How the king of Israel honoured himself today, uncovering himself today before the eyes of his servants' maids, as any vulgar fellow might shamelessly uncover himself!' (2 Sam. 6.20).

It is evident that Michal does not want to have sex tonight. Her words have a sense that David has publicly shamed himself, and as she appears in the story as 'Michal, the daughter of Saul', the distance between them in her mind is emphasized. Unsurprisingly, David loses his ardour and a classic row between spouses ensues. She flings in his face that he stripped before slaves and even the female slaves of male slaves. He flings in her face that her father Saul was stripped of the kingdom by the Lord himself, the same Lord before whom David was dancing in triumph. He says that he, David, will keep on acting as he has, valuing the honour given by female slaves more than Michal's approval. Many couples have said such hurtful things in the heat of the moment and made it up afterwards, but not these two – this row apparently ends the marriage relationship. What drove Michal's anger? Contempt for the son of a shepherd who acted in a very non-royal way? That is certainly how her anger clothes itself in her speech. David Clines thinks that her disgust is sexual – that her husband is flaunting himself, declaring himself available to anyone but her.[1] But it may be that there is something more than that. We will explore a reading that explains how the end of Michal's love story is prefigured in the beginning.

Bad beginning

It should have been a romantic story when it started. David, the young, handsome hero, was too modest to accept a king's daughter when offered one (Merab in 1 Sam. 18.18), but Merab's younger sister Michal falls in love with him. Yet right from the start this affair – perhaps a very one-sided love affair – is poisoned by politics. As with Merab, so with Michal: Saul has a political agenda in suggesting the marriage, one that will result in the death of David. Saul, fearing David as more popular and a threat to his throne, sees a way to get him killed. David's feelings about this marriage are ambiguous. The text tells us that he is well pleased at the idea of being the king's son-in-law (1 Sam. 18.26), not that he is delighted to marry the girl of his dreams. We are not shown a scene between Michal and David before they are married, and afterwards there is no speech between them until she tells him to flee. But we do have conversations and promises of *hesed* between David and Michal's brother, Jonathan. And so Michal's tragedy begins, for her bridegroom's heart cleaves to her brother and both David and Saul see this marriage with Michal as a power play. What can be inferred from his lack of dialogue with Michal is that David does not love her.

Role reversal

It has often been observed that if you look at Saul's two children, Michal and Jonathan, Jonathan displays what are often called the more 'feminine' qualities and Michal the more 'masculine' ones. Of course, for readers now these very categorizations are hugely problematic and rightly so. But it is reasonable to observe that Michal displays many of the characteristics that were admired in men in the Old Testament, and Jonathan many of the characteristics admired in women. Jonathan is self-sacrificing and self-effacing – he puts David first, apparently willing to put aside his own claim to the throne of Israel for the sake of his friend.[2] This self-effacement is a woman's role; he gives way. At their parting David declares that the emotion he experiences with Jonathan is more to him than the love of women: in other words, the tenderness we might have expected David to give Michal he gives to Jonathan.[3] Alice Laffey observes: 'Though in many ways her character has much in common with Jonathan's – a child of Saul who transfers her loyalty to David – she is never the subject of David's praise (cf. 2 Sam. 2).'[4] Michal, in contrast to Jonathan, is a woman of action. The text tells us that she loves David. Scholars note that usually when women's emotions are explored in the Old Testament, if they are explored at all, it is after the relationship has been publicly established or at least after the man has articulated his feelings. Indeed, Cheryl Exum observes that nowhere else in the Old Testament does it explicitly say that a woman 'loves' a man.[5] It seems to me that in offering this detail that Michal loved David before hearing about David's feelings, the author is telling us something very significant: that Michal's love is going to be exploited for political ends. Adele Berlin notes that David relates to her in a way that a man might relate to another man: practical considerations are the reason for his agreeing to marry her.[6] When Michal's father's soldiers come to get David she hides him and lies to the soldiers. She helps him out of the window in a way reminiscent of Rahab (who is the subject of Chapter 8). When David deserts her and then comes back to reclaim her, we are not told of her reaction – though her contemptuous comments when he dances before the Ark suggest that she did not meekly acquiesce.

Michal and Jonathan have one thing in common: both are willing to risk the anger of the king their father for David. Katharine Sakenfeld uses *hesed* to describe Jonathan's love for David: the willingness to endanger oneself or to engender cost to oneself for the person one loves.[7] This degree of sacrifice and endangerment is no less true of Michal. The ties to the family to whom one is born are very strong – we have an example of this in Samson, refusing his wife the answer to a riddle: 'Look, I have not told my father or my mother. Why should I tell you?' (Judg. 14.16). We should not overplay this, but when a woman is caught between her husband and her father, the decision to side with her husband is a momentous one requiring considerable courage. It is even more dramatic than a man siding with a friend, for a man can make a household of his own – in those times it would be much harder for a woman to do so, and a much more difficult life, financially and socially.

Jonathan gives up the throne and intercedes with Saul for David, so his *hesed* is public. Michal's *hesed* is in the private domain, as the sphere of women's influence tends to be – Rahab, as we shall see, can hide spies in her house; Michal can put a dummy in the bedroom. Michal does not defy her father in the public place of his court. Instead she plays the victim of circumstances, saying that David has threatened her life. It is hard to know whether she made that up for the occasion or whether he really did – a case could be made either way. We have already explored the fact that David is not portrayed as in love with Michal, so if it came to it he might well threaten her if she was reluctant to help him or afraid of her father. This might be the pivot point for Michal's love to turn to the hostility she later displays: their last contact is him threatening her life until she is brought back from Palti. On the other hand, she was very deeply in love with him so she probably would do whatever she could for him and there would be no need to threaten her. Although this explanation fits better with the picture of Michal as we have it in this episode, it means we will need to look elsewhere to understand what happens after David dances in front of the Ark.

Thanks to the ingenuity of both brother and sister, David escapes. David and Saul act out their rivalries in public and Michal is behind the scenes, reduced to the woman's role: waiting for her man to come home. And time wears on. Deuteronomy 24.5 says that a man should stay at home for a year and not go to war after marriage 'to be happy with the wife whom he has married'.[8] It is debated whether this means by building their relationship or providing a child who can provide for her if he is lost at war. Probably it means both. This episode shows us the consequences when this does not happen.

Second chances?

It might seem surprising that Michal is married to another man, Palti (1 Sam. 25.44), in a society where adultery laws are so strict, her previous husband is still alive and she is not divorced. But in the ancient world there were laws to free a wife whose husband had disappeared from her life. In Middle Assyrian law, law from a period not too far from the monarchy in Israel, after five years a wife whose husband was 'in the field' and not providing for her was allowed to marry again if she wished, on condition that she had no grown-up sons who could provide for her. Michal's husband has deserted her for a conflict. Of course, the prospect of living in caves with a gang of warriors, desperadoes or bandits – depending on your viewpoint – is not ideal for a woman. But it seems likely that some kind of rule like the Middle Assyrian law was invoked and her marriage considered dissolved. However, the same Middle Assyrian law also says that if the husband was prevented from returning by being kidnapped or needing to run away, or if the king sent him away, the wife had no right to remarry, and if the husband came back he was entitled to reclaim her. How did David interpret the probable practice of his time? Did he claim the king had sent him away (so he had, in a way, although the law clearly means on the king's business). Did he claim he had had to flee (as he had)? At any rate, he seems to know a customary precedent and he stands on it to reclaim the wife he left. The king and the law are intertwined as he is the last court of appeal. The system has beaten Michal and Palti. To make it worse, this marriage seems to have been a happy one. We cannot know that from Michal's viewpoint but we can infer it from her husband's reaction when he loses her. David settles at Hebron and insists on having Michal back. Palti follows her, weeping publicly (2 Sam. 3.16). A man seen to be weeping in public can indicate only an extreme expression of mourning. But his grief is of no avail.

The text does not allow us to know explicitly what Michal thought about being taken back by David. She might have been glad to get back to a man she had loved; she might have been sorry to lose Palti; she may have been, and most likely was, perfectly and bitterly aware that David wanted not her, but control over the remaining child of Saul. Her hostility to David with which we opened our discussion suggests that she hated being a political pawn. The Ark, after all, is a political tool too: the presence of the Lord who anoints kings is symbolized by its presence. This whole episode is about its arrival in Jerusalem and the aftermath. It is in this scene of political triumph that Michal's rage bursts out, and the argument between them is cast in terms of politics. Politics clouded Michal's love and heroism from the start and, in the clash of love and politics, love has turned to hate. She could have been politic, played politics and lived to be an honoured queen; instead she chooses to be honest about her feelings.

Judgement?

The ending of Michal's story is somewhat ambiguous: we are only told that Michal never had a child from that moment until she died. Some scholars argue that Michal is supernaturally made unable to bear children, that this is a judgement from the Lord. This judgement is seen as for one of two possible reasons: either for holding the Lord's anointed in contempt or to ensure the destruction of the Saulide line. Some scholars argue that Michal cannot have a child because 1 Samuel 13.13–14 means that there cannot be any Saulide on the throne: 'Saul's house threatens David politically and YHWH theologically.'[9] This is certainly one interpretation, but although it is made clear that the kingdom will not be transmitted to Saul's male line ('now your kingdom will not continue' – 1 Sam. 13.14), the prophecy goes no further than this. This reason seems unpersuasive. Although most of the Saulides were lost in the conflict, Mephibosheth, who is a son of Jonathan, eats at David's table (2 Sam. 9.10). He could father children and a man known to have the king's favour would be a desirable marriage. So we should not conclude that all Saulides are a threat. Mephibosheth is actually described as being part of the 'house of Saul' (2 Sam. 9.1) specifically. The favour shown by David is described specifically as *hesed* shown for the sake of Jonathan, who showed *hesed* to David. And the destruction of the house of Saul is not obviously at the front of David's mind when he goes to reclaim Michal. Had he simply been concerned to make sure that Michal and Palti did not found a family and set up a rival Saulide line, he would then simply have relegated her to his harem and made sure he never had sex with her again. This is what he later did, for different reasons, with his hapless concubines (2 Sam. 20.3), whose lives are then described as 'widowhood' – they are cared and provided for but never have sex with David again. But David, so far from taking this option with Michal, is clearly coming in from celebrating the Ark's arrival, to have sex with the wife he has got back – he might not love her but he certainly wants her. So it seems unlikely that David was particularly worried about fathering a child with a Saulide mother. He may even feel that forging a line with Saulide blood may strengthen his position. The terrible irony for Michal is that her rejection of David is what brings to an end her branch of the Saulide line. It will happen not through supernatural childlessness but through her own rage at how she has been beaten by a system in which women are always at the mercy of male power plays.

The other reason put forward is that Michal never has a child as a punishment for women who pour contempt on the Lord's anointed. It seems odd that this little lesson should not be underlined. The most likely explanation of Michal's childlessness is that the marriage broke down at that point – she rejected David sexually and so he rejects her sexually. This is to follow the logic of the episode, which is about sexual rejection. The whole of Michal's story is set up carefully to show the perils and pitfalls for a woman of offering and refusing love, and the dangers of politics. This is also how her story ends. But the end result is a terrible one for this woman: she never has a child and, as we have explored earlier, the role of mother is a defining one in this society. But if David no longer wants her, neither will he let her go: she is a daughter of a rival dynasty and could indeed be a threat in another household. So she stays, forgotten, in the harem. The system has beaten this woman of love and rage.

This story shows how women can get caught up in the politics of a system and have no say. Michal's marriages are determined by men and her fate by a power struggle between two rival houses. The author is writing her story as part of a succession narrative that argues that David is the true king of Israel. Systems are how life operates. But it is very easy for a system to become dehumanized and for people to become collateral damage. No doubt both David and the author thought that the stability of his kingdom was paramount. The author portrays all the dangers and complexities of the succession story further on in 2 Samuel as the kingdom is rocked by rebellions such as those of Absalom and Sheba. Rebellions lead to conflict and death. But this structure of patriarchy has ruined a life too. The author does not, in my view, criticize her but does accept her fate as a necessary part of establishing David's throne. Nor does the author challenge what happened. Michal's love story ended in hate and bitterness – the price of a man's kingdom.

For reflection

- How does the character of Michal come across in the story?
- Did you see any challenge by the author to how David acts and the fate of Michal?
- How do systems work well within the Church and when can they oppress?

7

Deborah: more like a man?

Judges 4—5

There have always been questions about whether women and men are different from each other and, if that difference is more than the purely biological, what form it might take. This raises for us a related and very important question. How does a woman operate in a situation controlled by patriarchal men? Margaret Heffernan set out four behaviour types that women in management commonly come up with as a way of coping in a male-heavy boardroom: geisha, bitch, guy and invisible woman.[1] It can be very hard for a woman to be herself in a patriarchal structure, even if she does rise to leadership. The types that Heffernan describes are assumed in sheer self-defence, but all of them involve the woman somehow not being fully the woman she wants to be.

Very often women who find themselves in positions of power find that they have to play down the fact of their being a woman to be able even to do their job. Queen Elizabeth I is an excellent example: she is said to have claimed that although her body might be that of a 'weak and feeble woman' she had 'the heart and stomach of a king'. Such a woman will have to operate in what may be called a male or patriarchal paradigm and may even be forced to do things that work against the sisterhood of women. This aspect of the patriarchal life, indeed, is not confined to women in positions of power. As we have seen, the Bible tells us of pairs of women who are forced to compete for the sexual attention or the approval of the same man to whom they are bound. This often destroys relationships, either between women generally, as we saw in the case of Sarah and Hagar, or even between literal sisters, as in the case of Leah and Rachel. But for a woman doing 'a man's job' the pressure to act 'male' is even greater. Such a woman is often accused of collusion in the very system that oppresses her. In the case of a woman in this situation whose story is told by a man, this would perhaps be intentional: the woman would voice the patriarchy in which she colludes in order to persuade the reader that actually, this system is what all sensible women want. Or perhaps such a male author could only describe a woman leader in the same terms as a patriarchal male leader. Instead of portraying her as a woman doing that action he may simply show her as a man doing that action who just happens to be a woman.

Of late the question of how to be a woman in a male-orientated setup has become important to the Church as more and more churches allow women in leadership. The Church is asking whether women's leadership is or should be different. If it is considered desirable to have a 'woman's' style of leadership, there is debate about what that might look like. People seeking to affirm women in leadership sometimes look to the example of Deborah as an encouragement. This chapter will explore the complexities of Deborah as role model and argue that she may not be such an example of non-patriarchal leadership as she may at first seem.

Complicating the issue somewhat is the fact that the story of Deborah comes to us in two versions: the older Song of Judges 5 and the later prose narrative of Judges 4.[2] Reading them together inevitably means that they will impact on each other and the way we read them. In Judges 4 Deborah should never have been in the battle and only came to be there because Barak did not trust the prophecy and asked her to go with him. In Judges 5 there is no sense that she should not have been in the battle. We will try to look at the two versions and see what they say.

The historical background is shared in both accounts. This is a time of crisis – although the nation of Israel is settled in the land of Canaan, loyalties between tribes are wavering

(Judg. 5.16–17) and the original inhabitants of Canaan are still in conflict with the settlers. According to the Bible, Israel's unfaithfulness to the Lord makes him stir up Canaanite or other enemies periodically as a reminder and a form of discipline. This time the cavalry army of King Jabin of Canaan, led by his general Sisera, has been oppressing Israel for 20 years. The Lord gives success to the Israelites and the Canaanite general is killed by a nomad woman called Jael.

Women at war

In the Song of Deborah, Deborah is described as summoning an army – led apparently jointly by herself and Barak (Judg. 5.12) – to a successful battle against the kings of Canaan (Judg. 5.19). Not all the tribes joined in the conflict, but the song seems to suggest that they should have done:

> Why did you tarry among the sheepfolds, to hear the piping for the flocks? Among the clans of Reuben there were great searchings of heart. Gilead stayed beyond the Jordan; and Dan, why did he abide with the ships? Asher sat still at the coast of the sea, settling down by his landings. (Judg. 5.16–17)

The leader of the Canaanite army, Sisera, seeks refuge with Jael (Judg. 5.24). After offering him hospitality, presumably to lure him into a false sense of security, Jael kills him by driving a tent peg through his head. In this version there is no explicit sense that Sisera is in any way helpless – he is not lying down asleep. Jael kills him in a confrontation. The Song ends with a triumphant prayer that all the Lord's enemies will perish as Sisera did; it is brutally graphic and to the point. Women seem to be accepted as warriors.

In Judges 4 Deborah the prophetess is leading[3] Israel at a time of crisis. She is doing a tough job in tough times. She is one of a series of 'judges' appointed to rescue Israel from the predicament into which its unfaithfulness puts it. The Israelites finally cry out to the Lord to release them. Deborah is given a command from the Lord for one Barak, telling him to go and fight Sisera and his army:

> She sent and summoned Barak son of Abinoam from Kedesh in Naphtali, and said to him, 'The LORD, the God of Israel, commands you, "Go, take position at Mount Tabor, bringing ten thousand from the tribe of Naphtali and the tribe of Zebulun. I will draw out Sisera, the general of Jabin's army, to meet you by the Wadi Kishon with his chariots and his troops; and I will give him into your hand."' (Judg. 4.6–7)

In this version, Deborah's role does not appear to be that of a warrior – she is a prophet who announces the Lord's call to war. Barak's immediate response is to say that he will not go without her. There are multiple ways we could read this. The most positive reading of Barak's reaction is to say that he wants Deborah as a sort of guarantee – that the prophetess who speaks from the Lord will ensure the Lord's help by her presence. Fewell and Gunn suggest multiple further possibilities: that it can be read that the 'spirit' she has received as a prophetess has also given her some kind of military skill; or perhaps her mere presence as the Lord's oracle will help morale among the troops; a more hostile interpretation might be that he simply does not believe her and, by asking her to go, forces her effectively to put her own life on the line for the prophetic word.[4] This need not be because she was a woman per se. The last of these readings is in many ways the most persuasive, as we will see below. The outcome of the story is well known: with the Lord's help, the army of Barak defeats the Canaanites and the general Sisera runs away. He finds himself at the tent of Jael, wife of Heber. In this version, Jael's actions are much more devious, for her husband is at peace with Sisera's king (Judg. 4.17). He is already weakened physically by his thirst (Judg. 4.19) and Jael actually invites him in and promises him safety (Judg. 4.18). When he is completely vulnerable because he is asleep, she kills him with a tent peg (Judg. 4.21).

In this version Jael then shows Barak the body of Sisera. The great significance of this is that it means Deborah's prophecy has come true, and it also reinforces the shame on Barak.

This is the significant difference in this version. In Judges 4 the role of Deborah as warrior is anomalous – it should not be this way. This story is designed to exclude women warriors as in any way normal. Gale Yee explores the idea of the woman as warrior and argues that in some patriarchal cultures the idea of woman as warrior is to create both an unusual figure and a calculated perceptual incongruity designed to shame the male readers. In this story, the women's actions are designed to shame the male characters.[5]

In most societies, war is a male province.[6] Women are perceived as nurturers, as non-combatants, as usually the victims of war and aggression. Yee argues that a woman warrior enjoys the privileges normally extended to this role in the male in his domain.[7] But in a society where the male and female domains are as defined as they are in the Old Testament, the woman warrior is a figure at the boundaries: 'She is thus ultimately dangerous and not simply because of her alleged bellicosity . . . she occupies a structurally anomalous position within the human domain and is thus potentially and actually disruptive.'[8] Although Yee argues that war in the period before the monarchy was essentially a domestic pursuit and women would be involved, it was not usual for a woman to go into battle. The model of Rahab (Josh. 2) would be the more usual way for a woman to be involved in war. A woman warrior, therefore, can function to shame maleness rather than to suggest that women can be warriors. In this way of reading, Judges 4 is an indictment of men who fail to be men. This is why Barak's refusal to go without a woman (who should not be in the battle) results in his losing the right (if that is the word I want) of killing the opposing general. Barak is shamed because a woman killed Sisera.[9] In the same way, Sisera is a coward who runs away and seeks the protection of a woman's tent. When a woman kills in this version in Judges 4, she does not kill as a man does, in battle. Jael's actions are not those of a warrior; they are those of an assassin who kills by stealth.

Overall then, if read this way the story of Deborah is not the celebration of a woman who can fight for the freedom of her people, rather a man becomes centre stage: a man who failed in his duty, so that a woman has to shame him into doing it by committing an 'unwomanly' act, and the glory of killing the leader of the army is lost. His execution is done in an 'unmanly' way. So far from finding a text that counters patriarchal structures we have found one that merely reinforces them.

Betraying the sisterhood?

Judges 5, on the other hand, presents us with a different problem. The Song of Deborah is especially hard to swallow from another perspective. Many would say that going to war to defend your home is at least understandable. Some might argue – although I confess I do not – that killing the leader of an invading aggressive army by stealth might be acceptable if necessary. But the language of the Song seems to take a particular relish in the fate of other women.

When Deborah sings about Jael killing Sisera, as we have seen, he is not portrayed as sleeping nor as helpless and unwary.[10] In the Song Jael becomes a warrior confronting an adversary. Fewell and Gunn argue that this makes the reader reconsider stereotypical views of how women act. But as they also note, the cost of this reconsideration is a painful reality. I suggest that the Song's picture of the usual role of women, waiting in fear and expecting men to rape in conquest, is the reality of women in a patriarchal society. In Deborah's time all this must have been the experience of Israelite mothers. However, the modern reader cannot resist thinking that no woman should take joy in such a prospect, and this is the problem of Deborah as character: 'A woman in a man's world, her voice hardening, merging with a man's voice'.[11] Not for nothing, I suggest, is this song sung by Deborah and Barak.

It has often been the custom in ancient societies for women to sing very particular types of songs for very particular occasions.[12] The Song of Deborah is a classic example of a victory song. But the Song does not only mock a defeated army – it mocks non-combatants and it mocks people with whom we might hope Deborah might feel some solidarity, namely women. The climax of the Song extends to mocking Sisera's mother, who has lost her son but does not know it. So the mother in Israel mocks a woman whose motherhood has been destroyed by another woman, Jael. The description of Sisera's death goes into some detail:

> She put her hand to the tent peg and her right hand to the workmen's mallet; she struck Sisera a blow, she crushed his head, she shattered and pierced his temple. He sank, he fell, he lay still at her feet; at her feet he sank, he fell; where he sank, there he fell dead. (Judg. 5.26–27)

This might seem unnecessarily ghoulish detail to us but it is important in the narrative of the Song. For Sisera's mother and her wisest women are portrayed in the Song as convincing themselves that Sisera is just taking his time dividing up the plunder. Sisera's mother is comforted by this idea: 'Are they not finding and dividing the spoil? – A girl or two for every man; spoil of dyed stuffs for Sisera, spoil of dyed stuffs embroidered, two pieces of dyed work embroidered for my neck as spoil?' (Judg. 5.30). The imagined violator Sisera has been killed, as Fewell and Gunn note, 'between a woman's feet', which in places in the Old Testament is a euphemism for genitals. So there is a strong overtone of sexual violence intended when death intervenes.[13] So the wisdom of Sisera's mother is debunked because her son the attacker has met a violent end himself. Deborah's song mocks the perceptions of Sisera's mother and thus the song has in it a 'reversal': Sisera's mother thought Sisera was doing this but actually this was done to him.

However, when Deborah puts these words into Sisera's mother's mouth, she describes the captured young women as 'wombs'.

In other words, in her song she has reduced other women –
albeit imaginary Israelite captives – to being slaves for sex. Few
terms of reference are more offensive to women than to be
referred to as merely sexual beings. That a female character
should choose to collude in this kind of offensive language
simply marks Deborah herself as a construct of patriarchy:
no woman drawn by a woman would talk about women – particularly women victims of male violence – like that.

All of this makes it especially challenging to appropriate
anything from the story of Deborah. Many of the attributes she
demonstrates are simply not congenial to a twenty-first-century
woman. This does not mean that we are not capable of her actions.
But most people – men and women – no longer believe gloating
over violence to be a desirable quality. On the contrary, we are
more likely to interpret it as showing undesirable qualities in
a person. To use feminist terminology, her story thus far might
well be seen as 'irretrievable'. In one account her story merely
reinforces the male and female role domains; in the other an
androcentric author has made Deborah speak as a man.

Is there then anything we might retrieve from Deborah?
She is described as the wife of Lappidoth; and scholars have
observed that since the word 'Lappidoth' means 'fire' we could
translate 'wife of Lappidoth' in Judges 4.4 as 'woman of fire'
– so Deborah is a prophetess and a fiery woman. The qualities
of strength demonstrated in a woman are surely to be welcomed:
it helps break the stereotype of women as weak, manipulative,
underhanded and consistently victims. However, as we have
seen, a woman warrior is deliberately drawn not to be the norm.

Prophet

In the way the stories are arranged, the first thing we know about
Deborah is not that she was a participant in violence but that
she was a source of wise counsel in Israel; that she was trusted
by her neighbours to settle disputes for them. And apparently

so much was she accepted in this role that she had a place named after her: the Palm of Deborah. The first thing celebrated about Deborah, therefore, is her wisdom, and there is no suggestion in the text that this is incongruous. As we have seen, a woman as warrior is set up in Judges 4 as anomalous, but her role as prophet is not. Throughout the history of Israel there were always women prophets and their ministry seems to have been accepted. A good example is the prophetess Huldah in 2 Kings 22, who guides Josiah about what the Lord wants him to do. Deborah 'commissions' Barak and sends him off to war; rebukes Barak for not trusting to his prophetic word; and tells Barak he will lose glory – the glory of killing the leader of the enemy army. As Fewell and Gunn observe, Deborah seems to be less restricted by the patriarchal society in which she operates – she is a woman who has authority over a man.[14] But she does not attempt to stand against those patriarchal values. One of the most striking things about Deborah and also Jael, the other woman in the story who shows herself as capable of violence, is that although both are married and referred to by their husband's names, neither seems to have a husband on the scene. Deborah acts without reference to her husband and Sisera comes to Jael's tent when her husband is not there, enabling her to entrap him. In this sense too their positions are at the boundaries: the male protector and decision-maker is absent. Nevertheless, in his absence the women simply perpetuate patriarchal ideas.

Speech

Deborah is a character constructed to uphold patriarchal views of women and authority. Her song is the song of patriarchy in its most violent, oppressive form, where women do not reach across boundaries to meet other women in sisterhood – they define 'us' and 'them' by patriarchal values. It is one thing to want to defend your home; it is quite another, from a modern reader's point of view, to sanction murder, rape and fear.

Language is a complicated thing at the level of shame and offence. The current popular phrase 'man up', as in, 'I need to man up and get on with it', might seem harmless enough. But its implication is that to persevere in the face of something difficult is a *male* trait. Referring to male footballers who play badly or exaggerate injuries as 'a bunch of girls' is worse. Taunt songs in ancient cultures would often compare male combatants to women. This is a patriarchal way of talking: it makes what is either good or normal, male. It makes women either inadequate in some desired quality or intrinsically other, not-us, different. A student once told me that I should not be offended at the use of the feminine metaphor for Israel in the prophets because 'C. S. Lewis says that we are *all* feminine in relation to God.' The student meant well, no doubt, but the implication of his words was that an undesirable quality is feminine; it is just that men become like women when they act that way. This is also true of the story of Deborah. There is a 'male' way of being that is normative; sometimes women can do it also but this is not to be understood as universally desirable. There is a 'female' way of being; when women step out of this way it is to shame men who have failed to be 'male' enough.

Heffernan suggested that the way to break the cycle of oppressive working environments is to model generosity and inclusivity to both men and women: 'We work hard not to repeat the sins of our bosses. We reject exclusive cultures. We may have been humiliated, stereotyped, trivialized, and marginalized – but when we build our own businesses, this is not how we treat others.'[15] If Heffernan is right, the way to be a woman in leadership is by being a human in leadership.

For reflection

- Is Deborah a construct of patriarchy?
- Is there a 'woman' way to lead?
- What examples of good Christian leadership have you known?

Part 3

WOMEN AND GOD

8

Rahab: living on the edge

Joshua 2, 6

When Joshua and the Israelites are preparing to move into Canaan, Joshua decides to send two spies ahead. He wants them to 'view the land, especially Jericho' (Joshua 2.1). The spies enter Jericho and go straight to the house of Rahab the prostitute. Some commentators have suggested that this shows how foolish the spies are since the first thing they do is not get on with their jobs but look for sex. In fact, though, a brothel would be a good place to go and pick up gossip, from clients or from the prostitutes themselves. Indeed, since in many cultures prostitutes were believed to be untrustworthy, they might have believed that such a woman would be more likely to betray her fellow citizens for money. The reality of Rahab's character will prove to be different as her story goes on. It would be fair to say, however, that the spies are clearly not very competent. Their one visit to the brothel is enough to blow their cover and the information they bring back is certainly of little strategic importance: they do not identify weak points or ways of infiltration; nor do they get to see a lot of the land. The only thing they learn is that everybody is afraid of them, a viewpoint they have been given by Rahab. The king of Jericho gets to hear that the spies are at Rahab's house and sends his men to tell her to bring the spies out. Rahab chooses to disobey the king's orders, hides the spies in her house and lies to the king's men, saying that the spies have gone. When it is safe she lets the spies out through a window, after making them promise that Israel will show her *hesed* even as she has shown it to them. She says she knows that Jericho will fall to the Israelites. They in turn promise to spare her and all her family if they are in the house. As the well-known story tells us, the walls of Jericho fall. Rahab is assimilated into Israel and even into the genealogy of David (Matt. 1.5).

Irony

Rahab the Canaanite is a woman who lives on the edge. She lives on the edge literally and physically since her house appears to be on the outer wall of Jericho. Her house is in a symbol of Jericho's strength. This is ironic since it is because her house is on the outer wall that the spies can escape, and it is the wall-dweller who understands that the wall is not as strong as everyone thinks. But she also lives on the edge metaphorically and societally. Phyllis Bird observes that a prostitute is contrasted to 'normal'; that is, 'married' women in patriarchal societies both spatially and symbolically.[1] She will live in a different environment and she will often dress differently to mark her profession (for example Tamar in Gen. 38). She is also different temporally since the nature of her work means that she will be out at night when other women are secluded away. The broader question of female seclusion is an interesting one. Tirka Frymer-Kensky observes that in the terrible story of the rape of Dinah:

> The very first word, 'out went', can strike terror into the mind of any patriarch. 'Out' means leaving the family domain, leaving both the protection and the control of the head of household. We often talk about the vulnerability of women who go out without protection.[2]

The reality of life is that women cannot be completely secluded away and protected. Nevertheless, the prostitute, who is free to come and go when she wishes, is different from other women whose movements are circumscribed in certain periods of Old Testament stories, for their own protection and that of their man's honour and prestige.

The male attitude to prostitution in this kind of society is born of an inconsistency. Men in patriarchal societies control the sexuality of their wives and limit women's sexuality to absolute monogamy, but some at least desire also to have sex with other women themselves.[3] So their attitude to a prostitute will be immensely ambivalent: they will have strict values about how women should behave and will therefore despise the prostitute as living outside acceptable norms, but they will also desire her. The Old Testament cannot be said to portray a prostitute as a threat, exactly. The prostitute is not the metaphor poets reached for when wanting to illustrate behaviour of which they most disapproved. That dubious accolade goes to the adulteress – a much more real threat to a society where families are defined by their male head, who controls the sexuality of all of them. Adultery strikes at the heart of this system. Prostitution does not present the same threat because it does not undermine any man's authority, does not run the risk that the children of his household are not biologically his; no other man's rights are infringed, there is no perceived threat to societal structures. There are some tantalizing glimpses suggesting that her life may have had more mainstream elements in practice. Jephthah of Judges is a son of a prostitute (Judg. 11.1) but also seems to be recognized by his family. Leviticus 21.1–7 contains laws forbidding priests to get married to women who have been prostitutes. If legislation is needed, it is probably going to be because the action requiring legislation is being practised. It may be, then, that in the time of Leviticus it was not unknown for a man to marry a prostitute. Prostitutes evidently were high enough in the community to be able to appeal to the king for a judgement (1 Kings 3.16). But a patriarchal society would distrust prostitutes, much as a modern one often does.

The unease about a prostitute who is also clearly a heroine is shown in early commentators like Josephus, who surmise that Rahab is an innkeeper. But as Bird points out, everything about this story suggests that she is indeed a prostitute. Her reply to the king of Jericho (Josh. 2.4) is couched in language that plays with allusions to her trade: 'they came in to me' and 'I do not know', as the Hebrew says, both metaphorical ways of saying 'have sex with' in the context of male–female interactions. This ironic speech tells us something else about Rahab, though: she is clever and appears perfectly prepared to lie to her own king for a cause that seems more important. Frymer-Kensky sees that Rahab in this respect is like the two midwives to the Hebrews in Exodus 1 who are ordered by Pharaoh to kill all Hebrew boys at birth.[4] We may also read a similar capacity for subversive humour. The midwives' excuse for not killing Hebrew boys as ordered is that the Hebrew women are 'vigorous', 'not like the Egyptian women', and give birth before the midwives can attend them (Exod. 1.19). The implication of this apparently innocent reply is that the weak Egyptian women need help giving birth whereas the strong Hebrew women just get on with it! Rahab's humour lies in the fact that she encourages the king's men to scurry away in a vain hope: 'And when it was time to close the gate at dark, the men went out. Where the men went I do not know. Pursue them quickly, for you can overtake them' (Josh. 2.5). In fact, of course, the Israelites are still in her house. Rahab's speech is full of a delicate irony that makes the men who deal with her look foolish – there is a degree to which she revenges herself verbally on people who have probably despised her.

Thinking theologically

In many ways Rahab is at first look that standard figure, the 'honest prostitute'. She is honest, keeps to her bargains and is apparently supporting her relatives or at least sharing in their lives. The somewhat patronizing preconceptions the reader might have about the 'honest prostitute' are undermined by her clever speeches, as we have seen. There is also a clear indication that Rahab can think, and act, theologically. We have already explored the idea that the Israelite spies might have thought a prostitute more likely to betray than anyone else, and Rahab will indeed help the Israelites who are her town's enemies. Her motivation is not money, however; nor is it merely fear. Rahab is a woman who can think for herself, who can reflect theologically. Neither she nor the other Canaanites presumably know that the Israelites have been promised the land, but she has heard about recent events:

> I know that the LORD has given you the land, and that dread of you has fallen on us, and that all the inhabitants of the land melt in fear before you. For we have heard how the LORD dried up the water of the Red Sea before you when you came out of Egypt, and what you did to the two kings of the Amorites that were beyond the Jordan, to Sihon and Og, whom you utterly destroyed. As soon as we heard it, our hearts failed, and there was no courage left in any of us because of you. The LORD your God is indeed God in heaven above and on earth below. (Josh. 2.9–11)

From this she can understand that the Lord of the whole earth can conquer Jericho too.

There are two verbal clues that underline how Rahab's thinking is profoundly theological: she uses the very significant term *hesed* as the understanding of her bargain and, as Frymer-Kensky argues, what she proposes to the spies amounts to something like a covenant. We will consider Rahab's *hesed* first. She shows her *hesed* by hiding the spies and lying about them. Frymer-Kensky observes wryly: 'Hiding and lying is the way biblical women demonstrate their loyalty.'[5] There is a certain irony that a Canaanite prostitute and the Israelite princess Michal (see Chapter 6) show their *hesed* in exactly the same way. But hiding is also something done by Moses' mother when Moses is an infant. Frymer-Kensky notes that the word used for 'hiding' in that episode and in Rahab's story is the same, and it is a rare word used only on these two occasions in the Old Testament. Clearly the author wants the reader to connect the beginning of the exodus with the beginning of the conquest.[6]

In fact the whole episode is full of language pointers to the exodus. The repeated use of the word 'go out' in different ways recalls the words of the Lord in Deuteronomy: 'I am the LORD your God, who brought you out of the land of Egypt, out of the house of slavery' (Deut. 5.6). 'Brought out' is in Hebrew 'cause to come out', hence part of the Hebrew verb 'go out'. In the same way, the king's soldiers order Rahab to 'bring out' the spies and she replies that they have already 'gone out'.[7] Aaron Sherwood notes that Joshua, in sending in spies when the Lord has simply told the people of Israel to go into the land, has failed to fulfil the Lord's command.[8] He appears to be hedging his bets, strategizing when he should be walking. Yet Rahab is in no doubt that the Lord has given the land to the Israelites, as we have seen. She is articulating a faith lacking in Israel. This is why it makes more sense to understand that this is Rahab's view rather than one that is shared all through Jericho. This is the personal faith of the person who will be saved because of her faith. It may be that the speech of Rahab is designed to contrast with the panic-stricken perspectives of the first spies to go into Canaan. The story of these spies is told in Numbers 13—14. They brought back a terrifying report: 'The land that we have gone through as spies is a land that devours its inhabitants; and all the people that we saw in it are of great size' (Num. 13.32). The Israelites then wanted to go back to Egypt and their refusal to trust the Lord was what led to the years of wandering in the desert. Frymer-Kensky contrasts their report – that the Israelites cannot take this land – with the report that these two spies take back, put into their mouths by Rahab: 'They said to Joshua, "Truly the LORD has given all the land into our hands; moreover all the inhabitants of the land melt in fear before us"' (Josh. 2.24).[9]

The second idea that conveys the degree to which Rahab can think theologically is the resonance with covenant language.

Covenant was a familiar idea both before and at the time when the Deuteronomistic History was being compiled. It was derived from an Ancient Near Eastern treaty pattern and was simply an agreement between two parties. It could be between peers or between someone more powerful and someone less. Covenant was made for mutual advantage. Where there was one party more powerful, the benefit would normally be loyalty and support with protection. Because this kind of treaty was a legal one in its beginning, before it became a way for Israelites to articulate their relationship with the Lord, there are clearly discernible elements and structures in a covenant pattern. A typical second-millennium BC Hittite treaty might include:

- a preamble introducing parties and historical rehearsal of past relations;
- stipulations;
- document clause (document kept in temple and read regularly);
- god list (witnesses);
- blessings and cursings.

A first-millennium BC Assyrian covenant – also a possible model for the biblical covenant – has similar elements. Frymer-Kensky identifies the following similarities to the Hittite covenant:[10]

- there is a preamble (Josh. 2.9–11), where Rahab describes her take on the history of Israel's arrival at Jericho and her conviction that the Lord has given them the land of Canaan;
- Rahab's stipulations (Josh. 2.12–13);
- the Israelite spies' stipulations, sanctions (Josh. 2.17–19: if Rahab does not follow their instructions they will be released from their oath);
- an oath (Josh. 2.14: 'Our life for yours');
- a sign (Josh. 2.21: the red cord) – perhaps Frymer-Kensky is reading this as related to the witness list.

Although these allusions are not a complete overlay of a covenant structure, they indicate two things: that Rahab's story tells us that Canaanites could and did become part of the Israelite community (as such, Rahab and other Canaanites who showed faith in the Lord are the other side of the story of the command to *herem* (the ban where the Israelites are commanded to destroy everything), as Frymer-Kensky points out); and that Rahab has been set up to be recognizable not as an 'honest prostitute' but as the faithful Israelite who keeps the covenant. It is astonishing how many times women characters epitomize an ideal: Rahab is the Israelite who keeps the covenant; Hannah is the faithful Israelite under affliction who turns to the Lord. The use of exodus allusions in her words suggest that in formulating her informal covenant with the spies, Rahab is seeking to become part of the saved community: as the Lord has a covenant with Israel as peer, so her covenant as peer with Israel incorporates her into the larger covenant. In this way Rahab is incorporated into the covenant community and this is the foregrounding of the text. The story does not consider whether she undergoes social rehabilitation because what is important to the narrative is not whether she begins to live her life within sexual bounds, but that she lives her life within covenantal bounds.

Trusting the Lord

There is a huge risk in what Rahab has done. We could apply the phrase 'living on the edge' in this sense as well. This is shown in her words to the spies:

> Now then, since I have dealt kindly with you, swear to me by the LORD that you in turn will deal kindly with my family. Give me a sign of good faith that you will spare my father and mother, my brothers and sisters, and all who belong to them, and deliver our lives from death. (Josh. 2.12–13)

She is asking for a literal reciprocation of what she has done for them: *hesed* in saving their lives. There is no reason why they need do as she asks. With the king's soldiers out of the way they can simply kill her and leave quietly. But their response – 'The men said to her, "Our life for yours! If you do not tell this business of ours, then we will deal kindly and faithfully with you when the LORD gives us the land"' (Josh. 2.14) – suggests two things: that the appeal to *hesed* is a powerful one at the theological level, and also that the author is making sure that the Israelites are portrayed as honourable persons who will be good to those who are good to them. It may be an intentional counterweight to the horror that will follow at Jericho. But the risk to Rahab has not ended. When the conflict begins she must somehow gather her family into her house (Josh. 2.18) and they may not then go out. This could potentially make them conspicuous, especially if her father or brothers are of military age and therefore should be on the walls. The Israelites may well spare her, if she lives long enough, but her own people may execute the whole family as traitors.

Bird argues that the entire episode of Rahab is predicated on the idea that she is a prostitute because the story plays with and subverts commonly held ideas about prostitutes. She says that the reader would expect no 'moral strength, courage, or insight' from a prostitute. She is viewed as a 'predator' – although she is in fact a victim – who preys on the weakness of men, and her only loyalty is to herself. She lacks 'wisdom' but is shrewd because she lives by her wits. It is not hard to see how the story of Rahab provides what Bird defines as the 'romantic antitype' – the heroic harlot. Bird argues that there can be no status change for a prostitute: she can only ever go from being a harlot to being a 'good harlot'.[11] However, as we have seen, Rahab's ways of speaking portray her not as the 'good harlot' but as a model for the 'good Israelite'.

We started this chapter by observing that Rahab lives on the edge. But the edge of Jericho is where the story focuses: it never moves into the town square. The walls are everything: Rahab's house is there; the spies are saved there; the town's defences are there; their defeat is also there; a covenant is uttered there by a woman at the edge of society. The physical, societal edge has become the theological centre of attention. Much has been said and written in the Church about reaching out to people on the edge of things. This story shows us that sometimes 'the edge' is in fact the centre. This challenges our complacency and an implicit idea about where the centre actually is. We may not mean to, but the Church does construct ideas about a 'normative' life that can make people whose life-profile does not fit feel very on the edge. Rahab tells us that thinking and speaking as faithfully as we can about God is where the centre is, not the type of people who are most prevalent in the group.

For reflection

- Could a woman living 'in the centre' have done what Rahab did?
- Who else in the Bible subverts our expectations?
- Whom does our society tolerate, and who is treated with double standards and some suspicion?

9

Hagar: look me in the eye

Genesis 16, 21

Hagar, maidservant to Sarai, has run away. A tragic story, Hagar's experience is a familiar one in the Ancient Near East. There was a common practice, regulated by law, that when a man married off his daughter he would give her a slave-girl.[1] If the wife could not have children, the husband could get the slave pregnant rather than marry another wife. However morally repugnant it is now to use another woman's body that way, Abram and Sarai do not see that they are doing anything wrong.

Sarai cannot have children, but she and Abram have been promised descendants by the Lord. So perhaps they begin to feel that the Lord helps those who help themselves. At any rate they follow the custom, and sure enough, Hagar becomes pregnant. So she, being probably young and definitely foolish, starts to crow over Sarai – giving a little of it back to those who have used her body as their tool. But there are laws about that as well. A slave-girl in the Ancient Near East who showed disrespect to her mistress in these circumstances would have her status reduced to that of common slave.[2] So Hagar runs away from the harsh treatment of Sarai. Then she finds herself in the desert. In Hagar's life she has had no rights, even over her own body. She is a slave who has been used as a womb – even the consolation of having a baby has got her into trouble. And now she is alone. The desert is not a safe place for a lone woman.

First encounter in the desert: the God who sees me

The text does not tell us of Hagar's religious beliefs. It is a surprising part of her story when the Lord worshipped by her oppressors, whose promises put the whole chain of events in being, comes to her and does not wait for her to call on him but begins the conversation. 'And he said, "Hagar, slave-girl of Sarai, where have you come from and where are you going?"' (Gen. 16.8). Questions in the Old Testament that come from the Lord are not about seeking information. In one sentence the angel of the Lord tells her three things: that he knows who she is; that he knows what she has been through; that he knows she is in trouble. He does this in three ways. First, he addresses her by her name. In a deliberate intention of the author, neither Abram nor Sarai offered her even that basic courtesy: they call her 'my slave' 'your slave'. They are set up as emotionally distant from Hagar. Only two people give her name: the author who remembers and records her story, and the Lord who speaks to her. So the first thing the angel of the Lord tells her is that she is not just a slave, not just a womb: she has a name, she is a person. Second, by also naming her enslavement, he tells her that he knows what she has been through; he knows what her life is like. Third, he knows she is in trouble because she is out here, in the desert, vulnerable, lost, hopeless. Hagar does not say where she is going – her focus is all on where she has just left. She is vaguely heading back towards Egypt, her home.

The angel tells her to turn back to Sarai and promises her a child who will give her descendants beyond number (reminiscent of the promise to Abram in Gen. 15.5). Fertility in the ancient world is a great blessing, yet there is more to this encounter than merely the announcement of a birth.

In the creation myth (Gen. 1.2–4a), part of the blessing on humanity is fertility, but it is fertility in the context of a blessing from God and a relationship with him. When God blesses the fish and the birds the text says simply: 'God blessed them, saying, "Be fruitful and multiply and fill the waters in the seas, and let birds multiply on the earth"' (Gen. 1.22). When God creates people there is something more. The text says:

> God blessed them, *and God said to them,* 'Be fruitful and multiply, and fill the earth and subdue it; and have dominion over the fish of the sea and over the birds of the air and over every living thing that moves upon the earth.'   (Gen. 1.28)[3]

So by including the phrase 'God said to them', this blessing is like a more intimate conversation, looking humanity in the eye rather than over their heads. It also commands that humanity play the role of God's caretakers on the earth. Both style and content mark humanity as relating to God. Humanity, both halves of it, is made in God's image and according to his likeness (Gen. 1.26). There is huge debate about what this might mean but what we can say is that something about all humanity reflects God. From the very beginning what sets humanity up as the image of God is not our ability to breed – although that is part of the blessing we are offered – but relationship with God. So the bearing of children is bound up in the broader idea of connection between God and humanity.

This same idea is implied in the Lord's conversation with Hagar: having first called her by name he then speaks of the child she is going to have.

> The angel of the LORD also said to her, 'I will so greatly multiply your offspring that they cannot be counted for multitude.' And the angel of the LORD said to her, 'Now you have conceived and shall bear a son; you shall call him Ishmael, for the LORD has given heed to your affliction.'   (Gen. 16.10–11)

Hagar's situation has been changed by this promise: the child she bears will be hers to raise. She will not just be the way someone else can have a child, she will be a mother.

Hagar responds to the Lord's words by naming him: 'So she named the LORD who spoke to her, "You are El-roi"' (Gen. 16.13). 'El-roi' means 'the God who sees me'. No wonder: she must have felt as though he is the only one who has ever really seen her – everyone else has treated her like a commodity, spoken about her and not spoken to her, used her. This One has seen her, the slave. Yet as many scholars have noted, all this positive experience is at least counterbalanced by the bleak side of the message the Lord has sent: he also tells the runaway slave she has to go back to the woman who treated her with such harshness. How could the Lord command a slave to go back to slavery?

Encounters in the desert: go back!

Some scholars such as Phyllis Trible have seen a sort of reverse exodus in this story.[4] Whereas in the book of Exodus the Egyptians oppress the Hebrews and the Hebrews run away, in this story the Hebrews oppress an Egyptian and she runs away. But we can observe here that unlike the Hebrews of the exodus, the Lord's command is not to leave but to go back to the oppression. This command to go back to Sarai and 'submit' to her uses the same root word as 'oppress'. This seems to imply that the Lord is well aware that when Hagar goes back her situation will be no better, but he is in effect telling her to put up with it. This is surely an uncomfortable contrast for us – the idea that someone would make a slave go back to slavery. The question is why the Lord would tell Hagar to go back if he values her as has been argued above. He knows what she is going through, he seems to value her as a person, yet he tells her to go back and submit to the very oppression he has told her he has seen. No reason is given explicitly, so scholars have explored a variety of explanations.

Some have suggested that part of the reason is that Hagar is not entirely faultless. She has treated Sarai with contempt: 'He went in to Hagar, and she conceived; and when she saw that she had conceived, she looked with contempt on her mistress' (Gen. 16.4). Trible is keen to see it as an exercise of some degree of equality.[5] She shows us another possible translation: 'Her mistress was lowered in her esteem.' Trible argues that a rebalancing of the relationship might have been possible here, leading to equality and mutuality: the slave-girl is raised a little, the mistress lowered a little. But if Hagar can see things differently, argues Trible, Sarai cannot.

Another view, one more explicitly based in a theological reading, is that what Hagar does is described as 'looked with contempt' – the same verb used in the Abrahamic promise to describe how those who curse Abram will be cursed. This should not be overlooked. If Hagar, who is pregnant, looks with contempt on the infertile Sarai, the argument goes that this means Hagar has done what was spoken of in Genesis 12.3 and 'cursed' Abram's family.[6]

> Now the LORD said to Abram, 'Go from your country and your kindred and your father's house to the land that I will show you. I will make of you a great nation, and I will bless you, and make your name great, so that you will be a blessing. I will bless those who bless you, and the one who curses you I will curse; and in you all the families of the earth shall be blessed.'
> (Gen. 12.1–3)

In my view a middle way of understanding Hagar's actions is to be preferred: Hagar is not 'cursed' for two reasons. First, a curse in the Old Testament tends to be very carefully formulated with a recognizable structure. Second and more significantly, in the immediate encounter with the angel of the Lord he does not speak of curse but, on the contrary, offers her two blessings: an encounter with the Lord and a son. However, it can be said that Hagar does treat Sarai as somehow less than she is because she, Hagar, can have children, and this could not lead to a more balanced relationship between her and Sarai.

She hurts Sarai at her most tender point and so Sarai reacts the way she does. But this still leaves us with a question: why must Hagar go back?

Some readings do not argue that Hagar has 'cursed' Sarai and hence become cursed but rather that it is important for her to stay part of the family. The readings also start from the covenant of Genesis 12.1–3, where the whole family is covered by a promise of blessing from the Lord. Such a reading works on the basis that Hagar as part of Abraham's family now comes under the blessing and therefore that must be better than to leave its protection.[7] These arguments about why Hagar had to return are based on belonging. Hagar is an Egyptian, but she has also now become a part of the family that will be the beginning of Israel. She will not be the last foreigner to be a part of the life of Israel. There are plenty of places in the Old Testament where we can point to a deep suspicion and dislike of foreigners – Ezra-Nehemiah is a good example. And yet here a foreigner, an Egyptian no less, is addressed by the Lord and given a promise of her own. In the Old Testament there is a clear strand that embraces foreigners who turn to the Lord. Hagar must go back to suffering, 'for the sake of what may follow'.[8]

On the other hand, another possible way to interpret the reason Hagar must go back is that in a story of patriarchy, everyone has his or her place in the hierarchy and Hagar's place is as slave to Sarai. Hagar is ordered back because she is a foreigner and under the authority of the Hebrews. She has no rights – she is, even to the Lord, 'Hagar, slave-girl of Sarai'. Trible notes that 'Hagar is powerless because God supports Sarah. Kept in her place, the slave woman is the innocent victim of use, abuse, and rejection.'[9] Hagar is finally sent away, argues Trible, not to free her from slavery but to protect the inheritance of those who have enslaved her.[10] This reading is a useful corrective to many Christian readings that seek to blame Hagar entirely for bringing her maltreatment on herself.

The author focuses not on the reason why Hagar must go back but on Hagar's reaction. If the encounter with the Lord in the desert seems a mixed one, Hagar does not appear to look at her situation. From the speech the author records she seems so transfixed by the experience of the Lord that she pays barely any attention to the promise given to her about her son.[11] In the same way she says nothing at all about the significance of going back – nothing about the fact that it will mean submitting to the bullying of Sarai. Apparently so caught up is she in what she has experienced, and reflecting on what she has grasped about the Lord, that her speech has nothing else in it but the wonder of the One who sees her and the fact that she has seen him and lived. This last idea about seeing the Lord is part of a frequent idea in the Old Testament, as we have seen in the case of Manoah and his wife (see Chapter 5). People are often fearful about encountering the Lord – in some cases they are afraid that they will die if they see him. In Hagar's case, she is not afraid but, rather, full of wonder that she has seen him and lived. Overall, if our experience of reading about Hagar's encounter in the desert raises uneasy questions, her reaction seems to be mainly one of wonder at meeting the Lord.

Naming in the desert encounter is foregrounded. As we saw, Hagar named the Lord in a way that expressed her experience: the One who sees. The angel names her son for her and in doing so gives her another perspective on the Lord: the boy is to be called 'Ishmael' because the Lord has heard her (*shama'* in Hebrew). So not only has the Lord seen her but he has heard her. This promise of a son also has perspectives on the Lord hearing her answer: when the Lord called to her, he used her name, described her slavery and asked her where she was going. Now comes a promise that builds on his first address and her answer (that she is running away from her mistress). The Lord does not free her from this slavery but does promise that the boy will not grow up as a slave; he will be free, not under anyone's power but equal to those against him. 'He shall be a wild ass of a man, with his hand against everyone, and everyone's hand against him; and he shall live at odds with all his kin' (Gen. 16.12). She is a slave but her son born in her slavery will be wild and free.[12]

When considering the command to Hagar to go back, Gerald Janzen describes Hagar as a 'first profile' of the suffering servant.[13] Trible, although coming from a different perspective as we have seen, also interprets her in this way: 'This Egyptian woman is stricken, smitten by God, and afflicted for the transgressions of Israel. She is bruised for the iniquities of Sarah and Abraham; upon her is the chastisement that makes them whole.'[14] We have already noticed that Hagar focuses not on trials to come but on the encounter with the divine. There is a useful insight in this prefiguring of the suffering servant in Hagar. It makes meaning out of Hagar's suffering – and suffering is surely the most painful of all realities and the most unbearable. In foreshadowing the suffering servant and Christ himself in the mind of Christian interpreters, it rebalances the androcentric view that Christ's undoubted maleness is somehow intrinsically vital to the fact of his being Saviour. By showing a 'type' of suffering servant who is female, this idea is corrected to a certain extent. It also solves for us the moral problem of why the Lord, the God who liberates, would send an Egyptian slave back to her slavery. It argues against accusations that the Lord is for Israel only.

The prefiguring is only partial, however. The suffering of the Servant in Isaiah 53 is purposive and vicarious – it is the very fact that someone suffers for someone else that gives it meaning. Hagar's suffering – whether she brought part of it on herself by infringing the Abrahamic promise when she looked with contempt on Sarai or whether she has done nothing to deserve it – does not do this. Had she kept running, Isaac would still eventually have been born and the story of Abraham's family would have gone on. Her suffering does not stand in for someone else; it does not release someone else from suffering or punishment. On the contrary, if she goes back Sarai will not have to face the consequences of her actions but can continue in them. In short, no one is set free by Hagar's suffering; rather everyone is caught a little more firmly in the coils of this family conflict.

Second encounter in the desert: hearing Ishmael

So Hagar returns, as the angel told her to; she raises her son herself, as the angel said she would – Sarai is not able to accept him as hers. We do not know if Sarai was any kinder to her when she returned. Eventually Sarah, as she now is, has a son of her own, called Isaac ('laughter'). Ishmael is playing with his little brother Isaac when the family are celebrating Isaac's weaning. He is laughing with the little boy. Suddenly Sarah can bear it no more and insists that both Hagar and Ishmael are sent away. Sarah's demand shows that she does not value Hagar any more than she did before, but on the contrary now sees both Hagar and Ishmael as a threat: 'Cast out this slave woman with her son; for the son of this slave woman shall not inherit along with my son Isaac' (Gen. 21.10). Hagar is still given no name by Sarah, only her status as slave. Abraham is concerned, but not about Hagar, only about his son: 'The matter was very distressing to Abraham on account of his son' (Gen. 21.11). Earlier in the story, when God repeats his promise that Sarah will have a son, Abraham's response to God is, 'O that Ishmael might live in your sight!' (Gen. 17.18). Abraham says not a word about Hagar. God's reply is clear:

> Do not be distressed because of the boy and because of your slave woman; whatever Sarah says to you, do as she tells you, for it is through Isaac that offspring shall be named after you. As for the son of the slave woman, I will make a nation of him also, because he is your offspring. (Gen. 21.12–13)

Even as God tells Abraham not to be worried for Ishmael, with a flash of divine irony he also tells Abraham not to worry about

Hagar, implying that he ought to have been concerned about her too.[15]

The problem is that God refers to Hagar as Abraham does ('slave woman') and tells Abraham to do whatever Sarah tells him. Leaving aside the fact that doing what Sarah suggests has rarely turned out well, by God's choosing to mention her instructions explicitly, he seems to have given legitimacy to her selfishness – it almost makes God seem as ruthless as Sarah herself. This time the question has changed for us: we no longer want to know why Hagar has to go back but why she has to go away. We might reflect that the cruelty of Sarah is so entrenched that in the end God is forced to take the least worst option and break up the family that would have been better together. Certainly human stubbornness can indeed generate a situation so toxic that in this world at least it cannot be repaired, because a person's hardheartedness can only be healed if that person chooses.

So we might be left thinking that, in the end, God did not care all that much about Hagar, except for the fact that God is willing to meet her in the desert one more time. This time, when God calls to her there is no mention of Sarah – Hagar is her own person, no longer slave of Sarah. When Hagar has no more water she grasps the reality of their situation and utters a cry of despair: 'Do not let me look on the death of the child' (Gen. 21.16). She moves away from Ishmael but God intervenes again. The slave woman and her son, of so little account to her master/husband and mistress, are noticed again by God. As he did in the first encounter in the desert, God begins the conversation. He says that he has heard the voice of Ishmael (although the text does not say what exactly was heard), just as in the future he will hear the 'groaning' of the oppressed Hebrews (Exod. 2.24). The last time in the desert, God saw and heard Hagar; this time is all about hearing Ishmael, but speaking still to Hagar.

This time God promises to make of Ishmael not only a nation but a *great* nation (Gen. 21.18). Implicit in this promise is safety and thriving for the child Hagar was afraid would die. But if God hears, Hagar sees: apparently miraculously, there comes a spring, which means nothing more or less than life. Here God has given the ill-treated mother and son a new life. This will be perhaps a hard life in the wilderness, but still a life. When Ishmael is grown up, Hagar will act like a father in finding him a wife – the usual role of a father. In the same way, in the first encounter in the desert the Lord is making the announcement of a son's birth to a woman – in all the other Genesis stories such promises are made to men. God looks Hagar in the eye; he does not treat her as an adjunct to someone else.

The significance of the spring goes beyond merely providing for their material needs. As Janzen also notes, there is an irony that the first spring theophany – appearance of God – in the Old Testament narrative is to an Egyptian.[16] In the exodus the question of water, springs and contact with God will be a vital part of the story. In the same way, a person who is the very definition of 'other', a woman and an Egyptian, has her oppression seen by God, just as he will see and act to release the Hebrews from oppression. In another few generations, another complete 'other', a woman and an Egyptian, will be the one who shows compassion and saves the little boy who will grow to be God's instrument of salvation for the Hebrews.[17] That story, too, will be a story about water. As always in the Old Testament we should beware of making global judgements of how the text views what is 'foreign', for here are two women who are foreign but who are seen by God as forming part of the narrative of his people.

So the tale is resolved in a way that has elements of the exodus account in it. Hagar and Ishmael are free from the persecution of Sarah – but there is no land of promise for these freed slaves.

The story of Hagar is one of encounter with the divine at its most inscrutable. We can attempt to interpret it as merely an example of a patriarchal, ethnically closed society's writings where the foreign and the female are seen as simply objects to be used and disposed of in the service of the chosen family. It would be a good reading at one level, but it does not adequately explain the encounter with the divine and Hagar's reaction to her experience of God in the desert. Or we can try to defend God by putting Hagar in the wrong, blaming Sarah or talking about covenant and promise, but as we have seen, none of these will quite do either. God sees and hears, Hagar is seen and Ishmael is heard, but to them is denied the privilege of understanding. Hagar is a theologian, reflecting on the nature of God, but she can only reflect within the terms her experience has given her.

Hagar's story is also one of suffering. Like the more frequently quoted example of Job, she is not given an explanation of that suffering. She can be said to be the voice of all those upon whom God has looked in pity and yet nevertheless not changed their situation, only helped them to face it. There are people whom God does not liberate from suffering and yet who encounter him and are changed for ever by the experience. For those of God's people who suffer the cruelty of others and are not given a reason, their mother is Hagar, the Egyptian.

One of the most terrible things about this story is that Sarai and Abram have not consciously done anything wrong. They have followed to the letter the rules of the patriarchal society that they know. The author seems to criticize the choice they make to have a child through Hagar but there are multiple interpretations of this disapproval: that it showed a lack of faith in God; that it forced God's hand. It is not easy to read the author's disapproval as a critique of the practice of using another woman's body as such.

At a theological level we might observe that although Abram and Sarai have not done a single thing wrong, they also have not done a single thing right. The absence of wrong does not make right – right is an outgoing positive quality, not the lack of something negative. This is why both Judaism and Christianity can never be legalistic religions – it is never enough in either faith to 'not sin'. Goodness is not merely a lack of sin, it is an active quality, transformative of all those whom it touches. So in a negative sense, for she has not been allowed to experience this outgoing goodness in her family, the example of Hagar shows us this too and challenges us to transformative goodness.

For reflection

- How do you think God saw Hagar?
- To what extent do you think Hagar brought about her own downfall?
- Hagar's story shows us that when we are utterly naked and without any other resource, that is the time above all when God can speak to us. Imagine now that God comes to you and says what he says to Hagar: 'Where are you going?'

10

Hannah: singing the songs of Israel

1 Samuel 1—2.21

Hannah is one of the two wives of Elkanah. The other wife, Peninnah, has children. Hannah does not and both the author (1 Sam. 1.6) and Hannah herself are clear: the Lord has withheld children from Hannah. We might hope that the other wife would be supportive but the character of Peninnah is set as someone ungenerous and bullying. We remember Sarah in the face of Hagar's fertility. It may be that Peninnah is a second wife, taken on because the first wife cannot have children and hence her motive is jealousy. Elkanah clearly loves Hannah (1 Sam. 1.5). The family comes yearly to Shiloh for a festival. Hannah goes to the sanctuary to beg the Lord to give her children. She promises that if he 'remembers' her and gives her a son, that son will be dedicated to his service. Such is her emotion in her prayers that Eli the priest thinks she is drunk and tries to remove her. She explains that it is only the depth of her emotion, and he blesses her. Hannah goes back to the family in a happier state of mind (1 Sam. 1.18) and 'in due time' – that is a way of saying it happened when the Lord planned it to happen – she becomes pregnant and has a son (1 Sam. 1.20). As promised, once the child Samuel is weaned, Hannah brings him to the sanctuary to live. Hannah sings a psalm of praise to the Lord. Every year she makes Samuel a new robe and takes it to him (1 Sam. 2.19). Three more sons and two daughters come along after Samuel goes to Shiloh (1 Sam. 2.21).

All about the man?

The story of Hannah begins in pain. We do not hear her voice until she reaches the sanctuary but before she speaks the author has told us a great deal about what her life is like. It cannot have been easy for Peninnah to know that she was not as much loved, so she uses the one thing she has as a weapon to demean her rival. In all the stories we have about infertile women humiliated by their fertile sisters, they are all the consequence of women being forced to compete for the attentions of a shared man: Leah and Rachel, Sarah and Hagar, Hannah and Peninnah.

Often a special time of rejoicing in the year is the biggest challenge to people who feel excluded from certain aspects of life. Hannah's story is set at a time of festival when there is a special meal happening. The role of food in the story is significant because it symbolizes the relationships between Hannah, Elkanah and Peninnah. The sentence about the food is rather difficult to interpret. It could read, and is generally translated, that Elkanah gave portions of the sacrifice to Peninnah and all her children and then gave Hannah a 'double portion because he loved her', presumably to make up for the fact that multiple portions are given to the fertile wife (1 Sam. 1.4–5). Or it could be understood as 'one portion *although* he loved her'. At any rate, whether a double portion or one portion lovingly offered, the food that Elkanah intended to use as a form of public honour becomes a symbol of the bitterness of Hannah's existence. He wants everyone to see that he values his wife whether or not she can bear children, but the relentless needling of Peninnah gets Hannah to the point where she cannot eat, not even this loving offering. We might see a story beginning in the way Leah's and Rachel's did: one loved and the other with children; both angry. But Hannah seems to feel only grief.

Elkanah's attempts at comfort are well intentioned. 'Hannah, why do you weep? Why do you not eat? Why is your heart sad? Am I not more to you than ten sons?' (1 Sam. 1.8). His speech

117

seems to focus on the marital relationship as valuable in and of itself and on Hannah as a loved wife despite her inability to bear children. Clearly he does not like to see her suffer. He is, we might say, a decent man according to his lights. But his words reveal his attempts to comfort her as also having a less benign motive than may first appear. It shows an important perspective on patriarchal thinking: the importance of children *for the man*. Once the man in the family has children, the problem is over. He has children so the family's economic future is secure. He has children so he is known as blessed. He has children so his name will be remembered through the genealogies, probably the closest idea at that time to life after death. In his view, then, that ought to be enough for his wife. 'Why do you cry?' can be understood as both a comfort and an implicit reproach, because of its co-text: 'Am I not more to you than ten sons?'[1] Had he been focusing on telling her how much he valued her he would have said, '*You* are more to *me* than ten sons.' The way Elkanah has phrased it, he feels that all her emotional needs should be met in him, that her desire to bear children became redundant when he had children. Pedersen argues that women experience joy in giving their husband children.[2] That Hannah should mourn when there are children who have fulfilled his need strikes Elkanah as inappropriate. It may be that her mourning shames him in a festival setting. His is the voice of patriarchy that focuses on the family as meeting the needs of its male head first and only of everyone else second. Elkanah is loyal to his wife but thinks according to his culture.

The lament of a faithful Israelite

Hannah is silent both when Peninnah provokes her and when Elkanah tries to comfort her. Hannah is a theologian: she knows that if the Lord is responsible for her infertility, it is the Lord to whom she must appeal. The fact of her silence until she goes to Shiloh is extremely significant in this way. She clearly feels she has the right to appeal to the Lord – if he has closed her womb, she does not appear to believe he has also closed his ears and his sanctuary. She does not approach as a repentant sinner, she approaches as a supplicant in need.

The progression from sadness to joy is played out in the public and private spaces of Israel. The story began, as we have seen, in the domestic, private sphere. Yet Hannah's pain is not only in the private sphere but also in the public. She belongs to a family with children, a family that, in the eyes of outsiders, therefore has what it needs to provide for its old age and bring honour to the father's name. Elkanah apparently treats Hannah with honour publicly at the sacrifice. Indeed, he does what he can to bridge the private and the public by honouring her publicly, and privately trying to reassure her that she need not be sad. In the seclusion of the women's quarters, however, Hannah is tormented by her rival and perhaps also by her own emotions, her longing for a child, perhaps even a question as to why the Lord has 'closed her womb'. When Hannah goes to the sanctuary, Eli the priest is at the doorpost, in a semi-place between public and private – not in his house but not leading worship. Whereas the public place was one of pain for Hannah, who wept at the sacrifices, this semi-place, in the presence of the Lord but away from both the community and her tormenting co-wife, seems a place where she can hold up her head.

Hannah goes to the sanctuary but does not make her prayer in a service, rather in some quiet time. The prayer she utters would be instantly recognizable to those who used Israel's psalms as their worship. Hannah is praying a lament.

O LORD of hosts, if only you will look on the misery of your servant, and remember me, and not forget your servant, but will give to your servant a male child, then I will set him before you as a nazirite until the day of his death. He shall drink neither wine nor intoxicants, and no razor shall touch his head.

(1 Sam. 1.11)

The public space of a service is not right for Hannah's lament: 'They [laments] take place not *in* the community but because there *is no* community.'[3] Hannah has no community: her husband cannot understand her pain and the one person at home who might have been a source of healing is driven by her sexual jealousy to be a bully. Even the priest cannot at first be a source of some fellowship to the grieving woman. Yet her words are familiar to the community as one of their forms of expression – Hannah speaks as the faithful Israelite under affliction. Her lament contains some clear elements that are also found in the book of Psalms:

- an address to God ('O LORD of hosts');
- a description of her distress ('if only you will look on the misery of your servant, and remember me, and not forget your servant');
- a plea ('but will give to your servant a male child');
- a vow ('then I will set him before you as a nazirite').

In other words, even those who cannot share Hannah's distress are still able to enter into it because the form she uses is one they will have used themselves in other situations. And when Patrick Miller writes that the laments are the songs of those who have no community, he is speaking of how they began. During the long tragedy of Israel, even these personal laments become the voice of communal Israel, lost in exile.

The worth of a childless woman

Hannah prays her lament with great fervency and Eli, seeing her emotion, reacts exactly as Elkanah does and denies her right to show her emotion. Elkanah did not want her to cry and also did not want her to fast. Eli misinterprets her emotional prayers as drunkenness. Elkanah does not think she is right to grieve and Eli does not think she should behave in this way in the Lord's house and tries to eject her physical presence from the sanctuary. In each case it is Hannah's physical state that is called into question by an overbearing male. Eli's rebuke is an attempt to exclude Hannah for it categorizes her not as a faithful worshipper but as a drunk.

Hannah's reply to Eli constitutes a direct challenge to his authority – he is after all the gatekeeper to the Lord's sanctuary. At the immediate level Hannah replies in a way that says both her body and her emotions have a right to be where they are (1 Sam. 1.15–16). But she uses a very unusual phrase in replying to him: she is not a 'daughter of Belial', as the Hebrew has it. This is usually translated 'a daughter of worthlessness'; that is, 'a worthless woman' (as in NRSV). This in itself is extremely significant because a woman who cannot have children is explicitly saying that she is not worthless. At another level the author is clearly deliberately playing with Eli's inability to control his own sons. In 1 Samuel 2.22 Eli's sons are called, again as the Hebrew has it, 'sons of Belial'. They abuse their privilege in the sanctuary by acquiring some of the sacred meat to which they are not entitled. They also profane the temple and abuse the women temple servants by forcing them to have sex with them. Old Testament worship was scrupulous to keep sex out of the realm of the sacred (see Exod. 19.15). There is a clear irony in Eli accusing Hannah, who is not a worthless woman, when he is himself the father of worthless sons. Eli's sons abuse the holy place; Hannah tells Eli that she is using it for its right purpose as she is crying out to the one who can help her. Other examples of those who are called 'worthless' in this way are the rapists of Judges 19.22, those who try to lure people away to worship other gods (Deut. 13.13–14) and the socially unjust (Deut. 15.9). So this word is used of people who are essentially considered noxious to their society. But Hannah is not noxious, not worthless – she has worth in the community. There is yet another aspect to the phrase 'daughter of Belial'. In later writings Belial comes to mean disorder, the force that works against the Lord's will, as the term is used in Psalm 18.4. So Hannah declares her allegiance to the one who can order and bring life into her life. And here in this semi-space, sacred but not public, Hannah finds her healing.

There is debate over Eli's words to Hannah when he blesses her. We could interpret his words as either '*May* the God of Israel grant the petition you have made to him' or 'The God of Israel *will* grant' (1 Sam. 1.17). The difference has some significance as it is the difference between a blessing and a prophetic word, a pronouncement through the old priest of the Lord's promise. It is perhaps a mark of how much he has recognized Hannah's intrinsic worth that he is happy to pronounce or at least hope for the fulfilment of a prayer he has not even heard. Either way this pronouncement is more significant as a way back to the private again. Hannah is comforted and goes back home to eat with her husband. The place where her anguish was most pronounced has become a healed place for her.

If Eli's words were intended to be understood as a blessing, Hannah does not yet know if she will have a child. However, although not yet pregnant, nevertheless her face tells of contentment, if not rejoicing. Somehow or other the encounter with the divine has reframed, although not yet solved, her problem. As we saw with Hagar, it is the encounter that has given strength to face what comes. If Eli's words were a prophecy it could be argued that the certainty of childbearing is what heals Hannah so that she can eat and drink. However, I think that the aspect of blessing is the more likely reading since Eli is acting in the scene as priest rather than prophet.

After lament, praise

We have already seen how Hannah's lament is a form familiar and used in Israel. When the Lord gives her the gift of a child and it is time to dedicate Samuel, she again speaks in a song whose ideas and shapes are very familiar in Israel. In the early twentieth century a scholar called Hermann Gunkel grouped the psalms in the book of Psalms into particular types. He did this by observing certain commonalities between the way psalms unfolded. A psalm of thanksgiving would typically look like this (with comparison verses from Hannah's psalm in parentheses):

- an introduction that mentions the Lord's name and may declare the singer's intent to thank the Lord (1 Sam. 2.1–5a);
- a recounting of the psalmist's experience (1 Sam. 2.5b–9):
- the state of distress, the prayer spoken in that distress, the story of how the Lord delivered the singer, a reference to the fulfilment of a vow (not seen in Hannah's psalm);
- a conclusion encouraging either the singer or the hearers to praise the Lord (1 Sam. 2.10).[4]

The next stage of Hannah's story shows how a woman whose life in the private sphere has been healed brings her healing into the public sphere. When she returns to the sanctuary, the semi-space in which she found her healing is no longer needed: she brings her son with a sacrifice – a public expression of her rejoicing. She proclaims her experience of pain, the Lord's answer to her prayer and the commitment of her vow, dedicating the much desired child to the Lord. Then Hannah sings a psalm of thanksgiving in front of the whole community.

Both Hannah's lament and psalm of thanksgiving tell us something very important about how her character is constructed: she is the voice of suffering Israel. Her lament contains no confession (sometimes they did), and this shows us that she should indeed not be seen as 'worthless'. But it also means that her songs together are the songs of Israel lost in exile and then delivered. The two songs together show that she is, in fact, a symbol of faithful Israel persecuted by enemies and rescued by the Lord.

Miller has observed that a psalm of thanksgiving makes very broad claims on '*a very narrow base*',[5] and this song of Hannah illustrates the point perfectly. For the fact that the Lord has given an infertile woman a son leads her to understand a good deal of theology. She learns that the Lord is incomparable and holy, he knows and judges actions, he overturns power structures so that the mighty fall and the weak are lifted up, he reverses life situations so that the infertile woman becomes fertile and the fertile woman is made weak. The Lord is the source of life and gives or withdraws it. He is the one who created the world, he looks after his faithful people and punishes the wicked. The Lord will be with the king.

This last is the most startling point, as there is no king in Hannah's time, which shows us that Hannah's psalm was put in her mouth by the writer of her story. But this need not detract from the significance of what has happened. Indeed, it makes it even more significant for it means that the author of Hannah's story wanted us to interpret her in the way being described. An experience of pain and answered prayer enables the character of Hannah to utter some profound theological truths and an extraordinary expression of faith. We have many examples of such expressions in the book of Psalms, of course. But when Hannah comes to pray her prayer of thanksgiving, in this very public space of the sanctuary, a form of worship probably led primarily by men and the proclaiming of theological thought are voiced by a woman. Even though the psalm is not composed by Hannah, the author has given this role to a female character because she epitomizes Israel at its most faithful. She is in undeserved trouble; no human agency can help her; she appeals to the Lord and has faith in him; she experiences contact with the divine even in lament; she is vindicated and her prayer is heard. Then she brings her thanks to God. So through this psalm the experience of a woman is given a stake in the psalmic expression of Israel.

The worth of a mother

For all her assertion of her right to be in the sanctuary, her resistance to overbearing male authority and her characterization as faithful Israelite, it could be argued that Hannah is merely upholding a male agenda in her desperate quest for a child. Yet Elkanah has told Hannah that not only is he not expecting her to have a child but also that he does not want her to keep on thinking about it. So Hannah's desire is not about pleasing her husband, it is about having a child for herself. By Elkanah's telling her she does not need to have a child for the family's sake, the author is highlighting her desire for a child as a desire for herself. It may be that the character of Hannah is constructed to show the choices and desires programmed into a woman of her time and society. Athalya Brenner believes that the choice to have children in the female characters of the Old Testament is either to propagate the social group or understood as 'the most essential wish of everywoman . . . women's motivation for becoming mothers is [re]presented as inherent, intrinsic, innate, inborn, instinctive, congenital'.[6] However, the rawness of Hannah's emotion suggests that the author was portraying what he saw as a genuine desire. The reader must decide whether we agree with Brenner's understanding of the author's intention.

Hannah is willing, without consulting the head of the household, to release the child from his commitment to the family and dedicate him to the Lord. One might interpret her desire for a child in terms of the status of bearing a child or defeating her rival because she is prepared to let him go after she has had him. Actually, Hannah's continued affection for her young son is shown when she travels to see him and brings him a little robe to wear, made by herself. When Rachel bore her first child she named him for her desire to have more: 'Joseph' means 'he adds' and the author tells us that when Rachel named him thus she thought: 'May the LORD add to me another son!' (Gen. 30.24). Jo Ann Hackett suggests that it is possible to read what Hannah is doing in offering the miracle child to God as an articulation of offering the first fruits in the hope of more harvest. Hackett notes that Eli certainly expresses the idea explicitly (1 Sam. 2.20).[7] So according to this reading not only does Hannah desire to bear a child whom she is apparently willing then to surrender to the Lord but she makes the vow in the implicit trust that it will bring her more children, as indeed proves to be the case. Or it may be another strand of theological understanding: the whole experience is about what the Lord gives. So she gives the child back to the Lord and yet loves him.

We saw that motherhood did not ease the mind of the infertile Sarah. She was jealous of Hagar when she could not have children, but motherhood made her jealous because of her possessiveness. Hannah has learned what Trible argued was denied to Sarah, the 'non-attachment' of letting go – nurturing the child faithfully in his earliest years and then symbolically releasing him to the God who gave him to her in the first place. Hannah is in a sense the healing of the story of Sarah when read in the context of the whole canon. She is not possessive and having a child is not what heals her.

Childless people in our churches often find the same thing on Mother's Day or Father's Day that Hannah found at the sacrifice. Well-meaning clergy encourage children to get a bunch of flowers for their mother or father and then to go back for more for all the women or men in church. For many, single and married, this bunch of flowers from someone else's kid becomes a bitter symbol of what they want but do not have. Or for some it is a symbol of what the church expects of them although they themselves do not feel the Lord is calling them to be parents. The pain of Hannah's story, the tension of private and public pain, challenge the Church. We do not mean to, but we cause pain when we gaily ask couples: 'When are you going to have a family, then?' There is not space to discuss this further here, but a deeper commitment to the Church acting as family to those members who are childless is much needed.

For reflection

- Does Hannah only want a child to make her equal with Peninnah?
- Is Elkanah well-meaning or controlling?
- How do we celebrate the joy of parenthood without causing pain to childless people?

Conclusion

In this book we have explored stories from the delightful (Ruth) to the unbearable (the Levite's concubine). We have watched what the author is doing and explored how the way the story is told can have resonance in our lives today. Most if not all of these stories take for granted the idea that a patriarchal society – where men are the visible authority structure – is how life is. However, within that constraint we have found that many of them also go to great lengths to give a full and often sympathetic picture of women.

One story, that of Deborah, really did seem to be androcentric: the author thought in terms of patriarchy and voiced a woman in a 'male' way. One story left uncriticized the structures of patriarchy that blighted a woman's life (Michal), perhaps because the author perceived the structure to be intrinsically important. Some of the stories took delight in subverting androcentric views by presenting women as the epitome of faithful Israel: Hannah and Rahab. Some allowed the subverting of patriarchy: Ruth and the woman of Shunem. Some stories overtly made no comment but I argued did criticize the impact of patriarchy on women's lives, if only obliquely: the Levite's concubine, Leah and Rachel, and Sarah. One story was the place where the broad question of God and suffering was expressed in terms of patriarchy and its abuse: Hagar.

So there are many types of portraits of women in the Old Testament. Many of them do not give us a straight teaching on how we are to live our lives. They do, however, speak of experiences that still resonate in our lives and so give us perspectives through which to understand our own walk with God. One or two gave no help from the author to find something that speaks to us an encouraging word (Deborah and Michal), but they are still worth reading if only to struggle with the question of what it means to be a woman now in a world that can still under-value us, think of us in male terms or think of us as 'other'.

Having walked through these stories I want to come back to my friend in the choir. A few of these stories are indeed andro-centric and fail to understand a woman's point of view. Most of them, though, revealed a more complex outlook. They should still be heard in our churches because they speak to us of God and his people.

May God who made daughters, and sons, in his image be with you.

Notes

Introduction

1 J. S. Duvall and J. D. Hays, *Grasping God's Word: A Hands-on Approach to Reading, Interpreting and Applying the Bible*, 2nd edn (Grand Rapids, MI: Zondervan, 2005).

2 A. Brenner, *The Israelite Woman: Social Role and Literary Type in Biblical Narrative* (Sheffield: JSOT Press, 1985), pp. 95–6.

3 There has been lots of discussion about this. Even texts that might originally have come from women, such as Ruth or the Song of Songs, would probably have had male editors.

4 Readers interested in pursuing this question are referred to A. Brenner and F. van Dijk-Hemmes, *On Gendering Texts: Female and Male Voices in the Hebrew Bible* (Leiden: Brill, 1993).

1 Leah and Rachel: such devoted sisters?

1 A. Brenner, *The Israelite Woman: Social Role and Literary Type in Biblical Narrative* (Sheffield: JSOT Press, 1985), pp. 95–6.

2 Brenner, *Israelite Woman*, pp. 95–6.

3 I. Pardes, *Countertraditions in the Bible: A Feminist Approach* (Cambridge, MA: Harvard University Press, 1993), p. 66.

2 Ruth: lean on me

1 K. D. Sakenfeld, *Faithfulness in Action: Loyalty in Biblical Perspective* (Philadelphia, PA: Fortress Press, 1985), p. 34.

2 T. Tanner, 'Appendix: Original Penguin Classics Introduction', in J. Austen, *Pride and Prejudice* (London: Penguin, 2003), pp. 368–408, p. 390.

3 Tanner, 'Appendix', p. 388.

4 Sakenfeld, *Faithfulness in Action*, p. 33.

5 E. van Wolde, *Ruth and Naomi*, trans. J. Bowden (London: SCM Press, 1997), p. 2.

6 Sakenfeld, *Faithfulness in Action*, p. 32.

7 Van Wolde, *Ruth and Naomi*, p. 135.

3 Sarah: made monstrous

1 *Inspector Morse*, 'Deadly Slumber', 1993.
2 P. Trible, 'Genesis 22: The Sacrifice of Sarah', in J. P. Rosenblatt and J. C. Sitterson (eds), *'Not in Heaven': Coherence and Complexity in Biblical Narrative* (Bloomington, IN: Indiana University Press, 1991), pp. 170–91.
3 Trible, 'Genesis 22', p. 189. It is worth saying that Trible finished her article by saying that this reading too must not be clung to as the only one.
4 D. A. Gunn and D. N. Fewell, *Narrative in the Hebrew Bible* (Oxford: Oxford University Press, 1993), p. 92, emphasis in original.
5 K. D. Sakenfeld, *Faithfulness in Action: Loyalty in Biblical Perspective* (Philadelphia, PA: Fortress Press, 1985), pp. 26–7.
6 J. Goldingay, *After Eating the Apricot* (Carlisle: Paternoster Press, 1996), p. 88.
7 J. G. Janzen, *Genesis 12—50* Grand Rapids, MI: Eerdmans, 1993), p. 55.
8 Janzen, *Genesis 12—50*, p. 56.
9 Janzen, *Genesis 12—50*, p. 72.
10 Janzen, *Genesis 12—50*, p. 73.
11 Trible, 'Genesis 22', p. 190.

4 The Levite's concubine: petrified of silence?

1 P. Trible, *Texts of Terror: Literary-Feminist Readings of Biblical Narratives* (Philadelphia, PA: Fortress Press, 1984), pp. 65–92.
2 Trible, *Texts of Terror*, p. 69.
3 Trible, *Texts of Terror*, p. 75.
4 Trible, *Texts of Terror*, p. 74.
5 Trible, *Texts of Terror*, p. 79
6 The Greek version adds 'for she was dead'.
7 Trible, *Texts of Terror*, p. 77.
8 Trible, *Texts of Terror*, p. 80.
9 Trible, *Texts of Terror*, p. 84.
10 First discussed by Noth in 1943, translated as *The Deuteronomistic History* (Sheffield: JSOT Press, 1991).
11 For a fuller treatment of this story the reader is referred to M. Bier, 'Colliding Contexts', in A. Sloane (ed.), *Tamar's Tears: Evangelical*

Engagements with Feminist Hermeneutics (Eugene, OR: Wipf & Stock, 2011), pp. 171–90.

12 Trible, *Texts of Terror*, p. 86.
13 Trible, *Texts of Terror*, pp. 84–5.
14 Trible, *Texts of Terror*, p. 84.
15 Trible, *Texts of Terror*, p. 81.

5 The woman of Shunem: independent woman?

1 T. Frymer-Kensky, *Studies in Bible and Feminist Criticism* (Philadelphia, PA: Jewish Publication Society, 2006), 'The Bible and Women's Studies', pp. 159–84, p. 165, emphasis in original.
2 C. Camp, '1 and 2 Kings', in C. A. Newsom, S. H. Ringe and J. E. Lapsley (eds), *The Women's Bible Commentary* (Louisville, KY: Westminster John Knox Press, 1998), p. 113.
3 F. van Dijk-Hemmes, 'The Great Woman of Shunem and the Man of God: A Dual Interpretation of 2 Kings 4:8–37', in A. Brenner (ed.), *A Feminist Companion to the Bible: Samuel and Kings* (Sheffield: Sheffield Academic Press, 1994), pp. 218–30, p. 227.
4 J. W. H. van Wijk-Bos, *Reformed and Feminist: A Challenge to the Church* (Louisville, KY: Westminster John Knox Press, 1991), p. 80.
5 Van Wijk-Bos, *Reformed and Feminist*, p. 84.
6 J. G. Williams, *Women Recounted: Narrative Thinking and the God of Israel* (Sheffield: Almond Press, 1982), p. 58.
7 M. Roncace, 'Elisha and the Woman of Shunem: 2 Kings 4.8–37 and 8.1–6 read in Conjunction', *JSOT*, 25(91), 2000, pp. 109–27, p. 123.
8 Roncace, 'Elisha and the Woman of Shunem', p. 124.
9 Roncace, 'Elisha and the Woman of Shunem', p. 124.

6 Michal: the thin line between love and hate

1 D. J. A. Clines, 'The Story of Michal, Wife of David, in its Sequential Unfolding', in D. J. A. Clines and T. C. Eshkenazi (eds), *Telling Queen Michal's Story: An Experiment in Comparative Interpretation* (Sheffield: Sheffield Academic Press, 1991), pp. 129–40, p. 138.
2 This not perhaps as completely self-sacrificing as it seems now. In Israel the kingship is in its infancy and it is charismatic – a

God-given gift, signified by anointing by Samuel at this stage. Since most other Ancient Near East kingdoms at this time worked on the basis of male primogeniture, Jonathan might well have expected to become king in his turn, but this is never a given in the text.

3 A. Berlin, *The Poetics and Interpretation of Biblical Narrative* (Winona Lake, IN: Eisenbrauns, 1994), p. 25.

4 A. Laffey, *An Introduction to the Old Testament: A Feminist Perspective* (Philadelphia, PA: Fortress Press, 1988), p. 109.

5 J. C. Exum, *Fragmented Women: Feminist (Sub)versions of Biblical Narratives* (Sheffield: JSOT Press, 1993), p. 43.

6 Berlin, *Poetics*, p. 24.

7 K. D. Sakenfeld, *Faithfulness in Action: Loyalty in Biblical Perspective* (Philadelphia, PA: Fortress Press, 1985), p. 33.

8 The Hebrew can mean 'be happy with' or 'make happy'. The Greek says 'make happy' and many commentators who write on this passage understand it to mean 'make the wife he has married happy'.

9 J. C. Exum, 'Murder They Wrote: Ideology and Manipulation of Female Presence in Biblical Narrative', in Clines and Eshkenazi (eds), *Telling Queen Michal's Story*, pp. 176–98, p. 185.

7 Deborah: more like a man?

1 M. Heffernan, *The Naked Truth: A Working Woman's Manifesto on Business and What Really Matters* (San Francisco, CA: Jossey-Bass, 2004).

2 It's reasonably clear that Judges 4 was written much later than Judges 5 – which is very old indeed – as part of the Deuteronomistic History.

3 This is probably the best way to understand the verb 'judging', since adjudication is only part of the work of Deborah and not part at all of the work of the other 'Judges'.

4 D. N. Fewell and D. M. Gunn, 'Controlling Perspectives: Women, Men, and the Authority of Violence in Judges 4 & 5', *Journal of the American Academy of Religion*, 58(3), 1990, pp. 389–411, p. 398, argue that he may be taken aback by the idea of a woman telling a man to go to war.

5 G. A. Yee, 'By the Hand of a Woman: The Metaphor of the Woman Warrior in Judges 4', *Semeia*, 61, 1993, pp. 99–132.
6 Yee, 'By the Hand of a Woman', p. 115.
7 Yee, 'By the Hand of a Woman', p. 105.
8 Yee, 'By the Hand of a Woman', p. 105.
9 Yee, 'By the Hand of a Woman', p. 115.
10 Fewell and Gunn, 'Controlling Perspectives', p. 405.
11 Fewell and Gunn, 'Controlling Perspectives', p. 409.
12 S. D. Goitein, 'Women as Creators of Biblical Genres', *Prooftexts*, 8(1), 1988, pp. 1–33.
13 Fewell and Gunn, 'Controlling Perspectives', p. 394
14 Fewell and Gunn, 'Controlling Perspectives', p. 395.
15 Heffernan, *Naked Truth*, p. 230.

8 Rahab: living on the edge

1 P. Bird, *Missing Persons and Mistaken Identities: Women and Gender in Ancient Israel* (Minneapolis, MN: Fortress Press, 1993), pp. 199–200.
2 T. Frymer-Kensky, 'Virginity', in V. H. Matthews, B. M. Levinson and T. Frymer-Kensky (eds), *Gender and Law in the Hebrew Bible and the Ancient Near East* (London: T. & T. Clark, 2004), p. 86.
3 Bird, *Missing Persons*, p. 200.
4 T. Frymer-Kensky, *Studies in Bible and Feminist Criticism* (Philadelphia, PA: Jewish Publication Society, 2006), 'Reading Rahab', pp. 209–24, p. 212.
5 Frymer-Kensky, *Studies in Bible and Feminist Criticism*, p. 211.
6 Frymer-Kensky, *Studies in Bible and Feminist Criticism*, p. 211.
7 A. Sherwood, 'A Leader's Misleading and a Prostitute's Profession: A Re-examination of Joshua 2', *JSOT*, 31(1), 2006, pp. 43–61, p. 54.
8 Sherwood, 'A Leader's Misleading', p. 49.
9 Frymer-Kensky, *Studies in Bible and Feminist Criticism*, pp. 210–11.
10 Frymer-Kensky, *Studies in Bible and Feminist Criticism*.
11 Bird, *Missing Persons*, p. 214–15.

9 Hagar: look me in the eye

1 *The Laws of Hammurabi* §144, in J. B. Pritchard (ed.), *Ancient Near Eastern Texts Relating to the Old Testament*, 3rd edn (New Haven, CT: Princeton University Press, 1969).

2 *The Laws of Hammurabi* §146.

3 Emphasis added.

4 P. Trible, *Texts of Terror: Literary-Feminist Readings of Biblical Narratives* (Philadelphia, PA: Fortress Press, 1984), pp. 13–25.

5 Trible, *Texts of Terror*, p. 12.

6 G. W. Coats, 'The Curse in God's Blessing: Gen. 12:1–4a in the Structure and Theology of the Yahwist', in J. Jeremias and L. Perlitt (eds), *Die Botschaft und die Boten* (Neukirchen-Vluyn: Neukirchener Verlag, 1981), pp. 31–41.

7 J. Goldingay, *After Eating the Apricot* (Carlisle: Paternoster Press, 1996).

8 J. G. Janzen, *Genesis 12—50* (Grand Rapids, MI: Eerdmans, 1993), p. 44.

9 Trible, *Texts of Terror*, p. 28.

10 Trible, *Texts of Terror*, p. 25.

11 V. P. Hamilton, *New International Commentary on the Old Testament: The Book of Genesis Chapters 1—17* (Grand Rapids, MI: Eerdmans, 1990), p. 455.

12 Janzen, *Genesis 12—50*, p. 45.

13 Janzen, *Genesis 12—50*, p. 45.

14 Trible, *Texts of Terror*, p. 28.

15 Janzen, *Genesis 12—50*, pp. 73–4.

16 Janzen, *Genesis 12—50*, p. 43.

17 J. C. Exum, 'You Shall Let Every Daughter Live', *Semeia*, 28, 1983, pp. 63–82.

10 Hannah: singing the songs of Israel

1 Y. Amit, '"Am I not More Devoted To You Than Ten Sons?"', in A. Brenner (ed.), *A Feminist Companion to Samuel and Kings* (Sheffield: Sheffield Academic Press, 1994), pp. 68–76, p. 75.

2 J. Pedersen, *Israel, Its Life and Culture, Vols I & II* (Oxford: Oxford University Press, 1926), p. 74, emphasis in original.

3 P. D. Miller, *The Way of the Lord* (Grand Rapids, MI: Eerdmans, 2007), 'Prayer and Worship', p. 203, emphasis in original.

4 This summary of Gunkel's work is taken from E. Lucas, *Exploring the Old Testament: The Psalms and Wisdom Literature* (London: SPCK, 2003), pp. 5–7.

5 Miller, *The Way of the Lord*, p. 212, emphasis in original.
6 A. Brenner, *The Intercourse of Knowledge: On Gendering Love, Desire and 'Sexuality' in the Hebrew Bible* (Leiden: Brill, 1997), p. 56.
7 J. Hackett, '1 and 2 Samuel', in C. A. Newsom, S. H. Ringe and J. E. Lapsley (eds), *The Women's Bible Commentary* (Louisville, KY: Westminster John Knox Press, 1998), p. 95.

Further reading

Bellis, A. O., *Helpmates, Harlots, and Heroes* (Louisville, KY: Westminster John Knox Press, 1994).
Exploring a wide range of women's stories and including points of reflection for readers.

Bird, P., *Missing Persons and Mistaken Identities: Women and Gender in Ancient Israel* (Minneapolis, MN: Fortress Press, 1993).
A stimulating examination of biblical texts relating to women, written in a clear and thoughtful way.

Ebeling, J. R., *Women's Lives in Biblical Times* (London: T. & T. Clark, 2010).
Using social-science disciplines, explores what life was like for a woman in Old Testament times from birth to old age and death, illustrating with an imaginary Israelite woman.

Frymer-Kensky, T. *Studies in Bible and Feminist Criticism* (Philadelphia, PA: Jewish Publication Society, 2006).
A collection of the writings of this extraordinary feminist scholar, dealing with gender, theology and the Bible.

Goldingay, J., *After Eating the Apricot* (Carlisle: Paternoster Press, 1996).
A series of explorations of biblical stories that also contain reflections from the author's experiences and his reactions towards the stories.

Gunn, D. A. and Fewell, D. N., *Narrative in the Hebrew Bible* (Oxford: Oxford University Press, 1993).
A clear and accessible discussion of how biblical narrative works.

Meyers, C., *Discovering Eve: Ancient Israelite Women in Context* (Oxford: Oxford University Press, 1988).
A detailed exploration of how social-science disciplines such as archaeology and anthropology have shed light on the life and times of women in ancient Israel.

Sakenfeld, K. D., *Just Wives?: Stories of Power and Survival in the Old Testament and Today* (Louisville, KY: Westminster John Knox Press, 2003).

Explores both biblical stories of women and their impact on women's lives today. Particularly valuable, especially because of its engagements with multicultural and global perspectives.

Sloane, A. (ed.), *Tamar's Tears: Evangelical Engagements with Feminist Hermeneutics* (Eugene, OR: Wipf & Stock, 2011).

A series of articles reading some of the more challenging texts about women and their interpretation by feminist scholars.

Trible, P., *God and the Rhetoric of Sexuality* (Philadelphia, PA: Fortress Press, 1986).

A challenge to re-examine some texts in the Old Testament that speak about gender.

Trible, P. and Russell, L. M. (eds), *Hagar, Sarah and Their Children: Jewish, Christian and Muslim Perspectives* (Louisville, KY: Westminster John Knox Press, 2003).

A series of explorations from differing perspectives from these faith communities.

Van Wijk-Bos, J. W. H., *Reformed and Feminist: A Challenge to the Church* (Louisville, KY: Westminster John Knox Press, 1991).

An open-eyed exploration of women's experiences in the Reformed tradition, challenging the Church to embrace these experiences.

Index of biblical texts